THE
Ultimate Guide ♥ to
Pampering
Your HORSE

Dedicated to horses

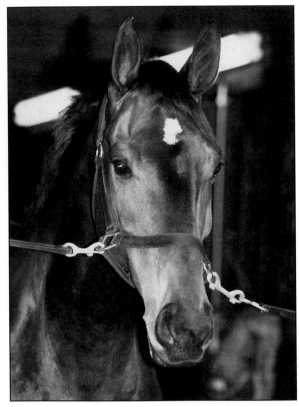

"The horses have to come first!"
—*Contributed by Anne Kursinski of Flemington, NJ.*
—*Photo contributed by Lynette Farlow of New York, NY.*

THE Ultimate Guide ♥ to Pampering Your HORSE

By June V. Evers

Published by Horse Hollow Press, Inc.

On the cover: Mary Ellen, the author's horse, is snuggly warm in her Baker Blanket jammies!
Mary Ellen is a 24-year-old Thoroughbred. She started as a racehorse at the New York tracks and then, because of an injury,
became a broodmare. I got her for free in exchange for taking care of her baby for 4 months. She has been shown (both equitation and
hunter) as well as hunter paced. She is retired now and is pampered beyond belief. She lives on our farm with Delta,
our 24-year-old Appaloosa, who keeps her company and receives as much love and pampering.
Cover photo by Blake Banta.

❤

Thank you to Jim Kersbergen, my editor, who has made
this book possible with his insight, wit and encouragement.

❤

Thank you to my parents, Bill and Helen Evers, and brother, Charles.
Thank you Lynn Borden, Dara O'Brien, and Linda Stark.

❤

And an extra special thank you to Blake Banta
and the Curvon Corporation, the makers of Baker Blankets.

❤

Another extra special thank you to J. Vincent D'Amelio
and Vapco, the makers of Pol-Cat Poultice, Fat Cat Feed Supplements and Bear-Cat Hoof Formula.

❤

Thank you to my friends, Darlene Williams and Joyce Groenendaal, at Green Valley Tack, Pine Island, NY.
And a special thank you to all the tack stores who believed in me before this book was even published!

❤

MADE COMPLETELY IN THE U.S.A.
1st printing: October 1996, 2nd printing: September 1999, 3rd printing: June 2001

Library of Congress Catalog Card Number: 95-078366 ❤ ISBN: 0-9638814-2-6

Office assistants

Table of Contents

"Lady, bring 'em in!" —Contributed by Kristine Gunther of Dousman, WI.

Foreword

by Kristine Gunter

*Y*ou asked me how I "pamper" my horses. I couldn't see how my ways would be different from anyone else's. I couldn't see what would make them special enough to be included in your book. But my mind played repeatedly with your question, and I watched myself with a new awareness.

I saw the horses' deeply bedded stalls, smelling more of pine and cedar than manure. I saw their "dining areas"—each with a wooden manger filled with fresh hay, a grain bin with its small measure of sweet feed, crimped oats and supplements, and plenty of fresh water.

As I tucked carrots or apples or dry corn-on-the-cob in their hay, I was aware that I delighted in surprising them. I was sure that many other horse owners do the same. I keep them warm and dry; or cool and wet—all as comfort dictates. I open and close barn doors to provide enough protection and plenty of fresh air.

Just like everyone else, I maintain their veterinary and farrier care, and keep myself educated so that I can intelligently continue their training.

Tonight, I saw that it was not a difference I was looking for ... it was a sameness. I felt compelled to answer your question nonetheless.

Lady, Mara, and Buttercup spent the morning in the dirt paddock. Last night's rain had made the pasture too fragile for their hard-hoofed shenanigans. The paddock was clean, supplied with fresh water, two salt licks, and morning and noon servings of hay. Two wooden ramadas stood to soften the sun's rays.

They'd had my company while I cleaned their stalls. Bug spray was provided with sugar rewards for holding still. Each horse had been taken away to a small circle beyond the pine woods for some mental and physical exercise on the longe line, and then allowed a bit of grazing in the lush grass outside the pasture before being returned to the dirt paddock.

Then I left them. They tried to get my attention when I returned, but I had too many chores to do to play with them. However, when the day's heat had sufficiently dried the pasture, I opened the paddock gate so they could spend their time searching for the very best things to eat.

It was when the sky darkened and the queer light and whipping wind sent me to the barn, that I realized how it was I pamper my horses. It was quite simple and probably universal: *I think of them first!*

They were in the far corner of the pasture. I opened the gate and called, "Lady, bring 'em in." Three heads came up. My proud lead mare flagged her tail. They popped into their stalls before the first drops of rain fell.

While the heavens roared and cracked, I had the security of knowing that Lady, Mara, and Buttercup were quietly munching hay. There is work to the care and spoiling of my horses, yet it's a labor of love. Their trust and responsiveness continue to bring a lump to my throat. And always will.

—*Contributed by Kristine Gunther of Dousman, WI. Kristine is an artist and writer. Her horses, Windmere Mystic Lady, MH Mystic Mara and Buttercup, live on her farm, Mystic Meadows.*

❤ ❤ ❤

An Introduction to Pampering

After creating THE ORIGINAL BOOK OF HORSE TREATS, I realized that making homemade treats is just a small part of pampering a horse. As I stood in the barn one day, fretting about bedding, stalls, turn-out, grooming (and everything else), I realized that there are countless other ways to pamper a horse. The idea for THE ULTIMATE GUIDE TO PAMPERING YOUR HORSE was born.

The call for pampering tips went out via the horse lover's network—and the response was phenomenal. I would like to thank all who took the time to send me their favorite pampering tips and photos of their horses. I've included as many as I could; I regret that I have not been able to use them all.

Mary Ellen and Delta, my horses, have thoroughly enjoyed being the recipients of tip testing. Mary Ellen's bay coat shines with dapples from hours of grooming while Delta, my Appaloosa, has luxuriated in knee-high bedding tests. They are both truly pampered.

Over the course of writing this book, I learned that pampering Mary Ellen and Delta is a way of pampering myself. Making my horses feel great, treating them right, and above all, taking the time to really get to know them, are all rewards in themselves. There's nothing in the world that can match the joy of owning a healthy, well-groomed horse and the warm feeling you get knowing they are happy and satisfied.

—*June V. Evers*
Goshen, NY

"My beloved Popcorn."—Contributed by Rosemary Speakes of Blue Haven Farm, West Milton, OH.

Olympic rider, Anne Kursinski, caught tenderly stroking one of her horses.

Sanchez. —Contributed by Joan Maynard of Vilas, NC. —Photo contributed by R.C. Chapman of Southern Exposures, Boone, NC.

Sonny and Riff. —Photo contributed by Ray and Victoria Wallick of Ellsworth, WI.

Important Note

Horse Hollow Press is proud to present THE ULTIMATE GUIDE TO PAMPERING YOUR HORSE. We're sure it will bring you and your pampered horse years of pleasure and enjoyment.

With regard to the recipes in this book, it is important to note that these are meant to be served as <u>occasional</u> treats, and are not intended to be substitutes or replacements for your horse's normal daily feed. And, while the ingredients in these recipes are foods commonly fed to horses, the publisher recommends that you check with your veterinarian first (as you should with any diet changes), and use your own good judgment, before you serve any of these treats to your horse. Also, remember to adjust the amount of the treat if you feed a small horse or pony.

When presenting anything new to your horse—toys, treats, costumes, etc.—always approach him slowly with it, and allow him to smell it and become accustomed to it first. Regarding the sections for parties and costumes, again, keep safety foremost! Nervous horses may become frightened and cause accidents. If your horse is too nervous, don't force him to wear anything he can't handle. And remember always to incorporate a hard hat into the design of your own costume. While many of the contributed photos in this book show riders without hard hats, Horse Hollow Press strongly urges all riders to wear hard hats, at all times, when riding.

With these recommendations in mind, it is our pleasure to share with you what other horse lovers from all over the United States and Canada have so generously shared with us. These fabulous pampering tips and recipes are so much fun—and your horse will absolutely love them (and you)! Enjoy!

—*Horse Hollow Press, Inc.*
Goshen, NY

—*Photo contributed by The American Paint Horse Association of Fort Worth, TX.*

—*Photo contributed by The International Arabian Horse Association of Denver, CO. Photo by Johnny Johnston.*

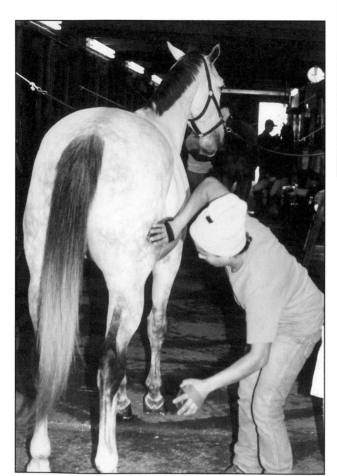

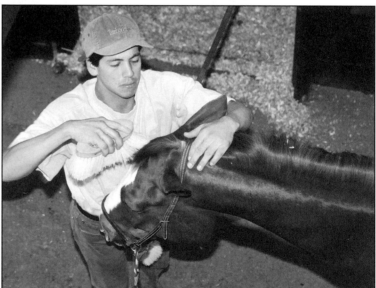

"At Hunterdon, we wear out grooming mitts in two weeks. Each horse is groomed for one hour or more every day."
—Contributed by Jennifer Bates, barn manager of George Morris' Hunterdon Farms, Pittstown, NJ.
—Photos contributed by Lynette Farlow of New York, NY.

Ultimate
GROOMING

*"I keep pictures of my husband and my horse at work—
the horse's picture is always much larger!"
—Contributed by Patricia Noonan of Naperville, IL.*

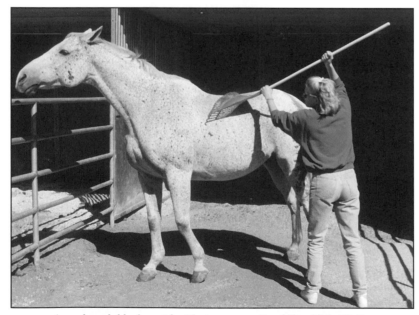

*A much-needed back scratch with an unconventional "brush" that Bobby,
a French Anglo-Arab, loves!—Photo contributed by Amber Scheidt of West Jordan, UT.*

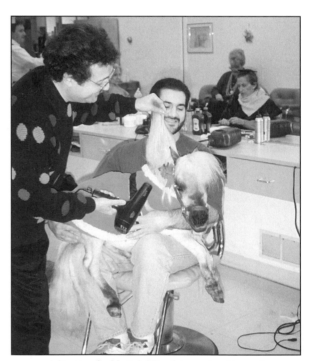

*Adieu to a bad hairdo! Penelope receives the royal
treatment in a salon.—Photo contributed by Sandy Larkin
of Webster, NY. Note the woman in the background mirror:
she doesn't seem to notice anything amiss—as if a small
horse getting primped in a salon chair is business as
usual at Alfredo's!*

8-Step Leave 'em Gleamin' Grooming

1

Materials:

- 2 dandy or stiff brushes
- Rubber curry comb
- Plastic curry comb
- 2 rubber grooming mitts
- Body brush
- Soft brush
- Human hairbrush
- 2 towels

2

Brush all large areas free of loose dirt, hair, and caked-on mud with a dandy or stiff brush. (This brush will get very dirty, so use it only for this initial brushing.)

Brush in the direction of the hair, starting at the top of the neck and working your way back to the hindquarters. Brush the legs all the way down to the feet, knocking off any mud dried to the fetlocks (ankles) and around the coronet band (rim of hair where the hoof begins).

3

Then, use a rubber curry comb and groom vigorously in small circles (currying). Currying removes deep-down dirt, dried skin, and hair while also massaging the muscles.

Start high on the neck, currying the horse's entire body except his face and legs. Press more firmly on meaty areas, such as hindquarters, and lighter over bonier areas (where it could hurt). Tap out the dirt frequently from the curry comb.

Next, use a plastic curry comb to curry first in small circles, then in the direction of the hair. The harder teeth of the comb help push out even more dirt and hair.

Silver Bullet. —Photo contributed by Jess Johnson of Tack on Wheels Store, Winston-Salem, NC.

Super Suggestion:

♥ **Give him a daily shine.** For the ultimate glistening coat, nothing can replace a daily grooming. It is the single best conditioner for stimulating natural oils and bringing out the shine in his coat.

"Pod gives me a kiss." —Contributed by Kathryn Lauren of West River, MD. Pod is her 13-year-old Thoroughbred. —Photo by R. James Chaconas of Rockville, MD.

8-Step Leave 'em Gleamin' Grooming

4

Then, put on a rubber grooming mitt and gently rub the horse's entire face. Carefully massage the forehead, around the eyes and ears, under the jaw in between the jawbones, and around the throatlatch area.

5

Wear grooming mitts on both hands to groom legs. Press both hands flat against each side of the leg, and curry vigorously with an alternating up and down motion. Curry the entire leg, around knees, hocks and tendons. Use your mitted fingers to scrub in recesses and curves. Pay attention to the area around the coronet band and behind the pastern (right above heels at the back of the ankles) where dirt can accumulate. This is excellent for massaging tendons and ankles.

Mary Ellen's Corner
NEVER kneel on the ground to work on a horse's legs. I bend over or squat whenever I work on Mary Ellen's legs and stay out of range should she kick or strike out. Safety and caution is always first!

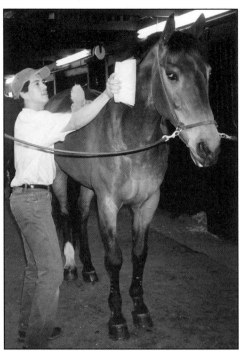

"To me, this is normal care! It's pride in my horse's appearance. There is nothing I'd rather spend my energy on." —Contributed by Anita Cantor of Scottsdale, AZ. —Photos contributed by Lynette Farlow of New York, NY.

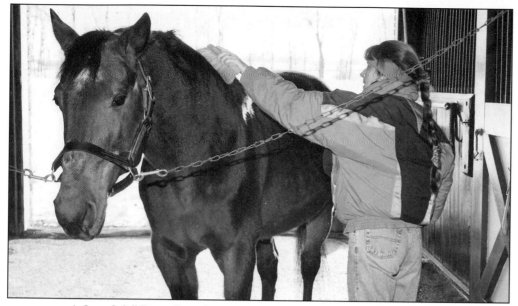

At Lana Lobell Farms, Dawn Lyons grooms 28-year-old Speedy Crown, the leading sire of trotting Standardbred racehorses. —Photo contributed by Judy Decker of Johnson, NY.

6

Next, use a fresh dandy or stiff brush and brush the entire horse except the face (this brush will be too harsh). Include legs and behind pasterns. Brush in the direction of the hair, using a firm stroke. Snap the brush up and away from you at the end of the stroke to whisk the dirt off the horse.

Next, use a body brush (which is softer than a dandy brush) to brush the entire horse in the direction of the hair. Include the face. Frequently clean the dust out of the brush by brushing it against a curry comb. This will keep the brush actively working to pick up as much dust as possible without putting it back into the horse.

Then, with an even finer, softer brush (the softer, the better!), brush the entire horse in the direction of the hair. Again, clean out the brush frequently.

Super Suggestions:

❤ **Scale back the chestnuts.** Chestnuts are scaly growths on the inside of all four legs. They usually take care of themselves by falling off naturally. For a little extra pampering, rub a dab of petroleum jelly or mineral oil into chestnuts. This will help them drop off on their own or allow you to carefully peel off loose pieces yourself.

❤ **Ease off the ergots.** Ergots are the small horny growths at the bottom of the fetlock. Rub in a non-greasy moisturizer, such as Nolvasan, (petroleum jelly will attract too much dirt), and they will fall off on their own.

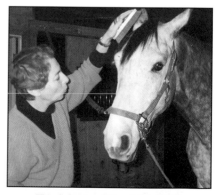

"I indulge myself in giving Peppie a complete grooming!"—Contributed by Beth Ann Adams of Bethlehem, PA.

Super Suggestions:

- **Spring for sheepskin luxury.** For a luxurious finishing touch, wipe your horse off with a sheepskin polishing mitt instead of a towel. Spray a little conditioner directly on the mitt and rub in well for a real shine.

- **Concoct your own conditioning.** Instead of spray-on conditioner, mix equal parts cider vinegar, baby oil, and Listerine together in a spray bottle. Spray it on a terry cloth towel and rub into horse's coat.

- **Add the baby-soft touch.** Rinse a towel in a bucket of water and a little baby oil. Let towel air dry and then use it for the final rub down.

8-Step Leave 'em Gleamin' Grooming

7

Use a human hair brush to brush the mane. First, flip it over to the other side of the neck and brush thoroughly. Return it to the regular side, dampen the brush, and brush through one more time.

For the tail, use the same brush (or a dandy or body brush will do). Start at the bottom of the tail and brush very gently to work tangles out. Slowly untangle your way up to the top of the tail. Ripping the brush through the tail will tear hairs out and create an unkempt-looking tail. If the tail is very tangled, spray on some conditioner and gently work the tangles loose with your fingers before continuing to brush.

Mary Ellen's Corner
You may choose to pick out your horse's tail by hand, instead of brushing, to keep hairs from tearing out. I prefer to brush Mary Ellen's tail gently with a human hair brush or dandy brush. I like the fluffy, brushed look it creates.

8

Then, wipe off any remaining dust with a towel. Mist the towel lightly with water or spray-on conditioner to pick up any stubborn dust particles left.

Dampen the towel with warm water and clean under the tail, around the sheath or the udders, and between the hind legs. Pick up a fresh, damp towel and carefully wipe around eyes and nostrils.

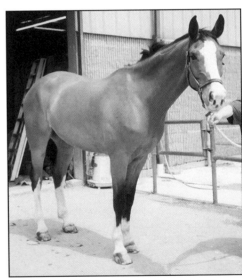

Then, stand back and look at him shine! Here's Baron at Overpeck Farms, Leonia, NJ.—Photo contributed by Joyce Chorbajian of New York, NY.

There's More!

Extra Vigorous Back & Hindquarter Treatment

Curry in tiny, firm circles over the saddle area of the back and the entire hindquarters with a Grooma Groomer, the large black rubber Grooma. As you massage this area, your horse will tell you the amount of pressure that is comfortable for him. Always groom with lighter pressure over the kidneys (area right behind the saddle). Brush loosened dirt and hair off with a body brush.

If your horse tends to be more sensitive, use the Grooma Soft Touch Brush (a gentler version of the Grooma Groomer).

Mary Ellen's Corner
In the winter when her coat is thicker, Mary Ellen loves this vigorous grooming. In the summer, however, her skin and thinner coat are too sensitive. I use the smaller, softer Grooma.

"What a Relief!" Shedding Pre-Groom

A shedding blade has two sides: the smooth side to be used as a sweat scraper, and the serrated side to help pull out shedding hair. In the spring, you can help your horse shed out faster by using the serated edge flat, not looped, and scraping in the direction of the hair over the meaty, muscled parts of the horse. (Do not use it over the bony surfaces.)

Scrape energetically to loosen hair and remove dirt and dander. Shedding hair is itchy, so your horse will really enjoy this. Then, follow with the full grooming.

Static Cling Solution

Sew three sides of a prefolded cloth diaper closed, and insert a dryer sheet inside. Rub your horse in the direction of the hair to eliminate the static electricity in his coat and also pick up fine dust particles. You can also sew velcro into the open end to keep the dryer sheet inside. Replace the dryer sheet as needed.

—Contributed by June Laughlin of Bedford, VA.

Super Suggestions:

❤ **Brush up on brush care.** Every other month, you should wash your brushes in warm water and soap. Dunk brushes with wooden or plastic parts into soapy water. Rub them vigorously against a curry comb to get all the dirt out, and rinse thoroughly. Let them sit in the sun to dry.

❤ **Make your leather last forever.** Do not dunk your leather brushes. Clean them by brushing vigorously against a clean curry comb and then wiping the bristles with a damp sponge. Clean the leather parts with a leather cleaner and moisturizer.

—Photo contributed by Lisa Allen, creative director of Hunter & Sport Horse, Ft. Wayne, IN.

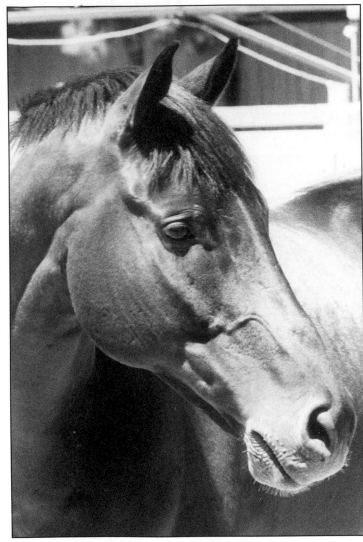

—Photo contributed by
Kris Bagwell of Quincy, CA.

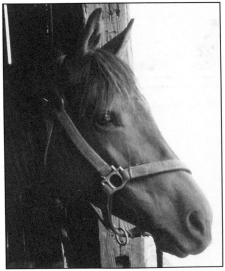

Chaps. —Photo contributed by Ellie Powers
of Eldersburg, MD.

Special Bargain, a 9-year-old Thoroughbred, is an adopted former racehorse.
—Photo contributed by Beth Lincoln of Rancho Santa Margarita, CA.

"Putting your face up to his head and neck, it's such a nice clean smell. Even his breath has a clean smell ..." —Contributed by Sam Savitt of North Salem, NY. —Photo contributed by Mary Ann O'Keefe of Whip N Spur Catalog & Tack Shop, Tampa, FL.

Faces

Extra Special Face Grooming

Materials:

> Grooming halter
> Grooma Soft Touch Brush
> Extra soft brush
> Chamois cloth

Change your horse into his grooming halter and cross-tie him. (A grooming halter makes grooming easier because it lacks the extra throat latch strap that blocks the cheek surface.)

Curry the entire face very gently with the Grooma brush, using small gentle circles. Pay particular attention to the skin under the eyes where dried sweat and dirt can collect. Then, curry around and between the ears and around his forelock.

Pick up the soft brush and brush in the direction of the hair. Spend 5 - 10 minutes just brushing the entire face softly.

Use only a slightly firmer stroke over the muscles in the forehead and cheeks.

Next, pick up a clean chamois cloth and wrap the loose end of the cloth around your hand so the excess will not flap in his face. Slowly and gently, wipe his face to smooth the hair down.

Then, rub the face in the direction of the hair with your bare hands, smoothing off all dust. When you run your hands over his eyes, he will shut them. Smooth the hair down and cup your hands over his eyes. Talk softly to him. It is very soothing and creates trust between you.

Mary Ellen's Corner
Mary Ellen, a Thoroughbred off the race track, was terribly head shy when we first got her. I spent a lot of time just carefully grooming her face, talking to her, and encouraging her to put her head down. Now whenever I rub the hair over her eyelids and gently cup my hands over her closed eyes, she immediately relaxes. **Remember:** when trying new tips, do them slowly and never use force. You will always create trust through gentleness.

Super Suggestions:

- ♥ **Be extra gentle with the extra sensitive.** For extra gentle brushing, try a Be Gentle Face Brush. It's a tiny 4-inch brush with small, soft bristles made especially for faces.

- ♥ **Keep 'em kissing clean.** Clean his muzzle and nostrils with Baby Wipes. It leaves them sweet smelling—important because that's where we kiss them!
  —*Contributed by Beth Lincoln of Rancho Santa Margarita, CA.*

—*Photo contributed by Lynette Farlow of New York, NY. Lynette is a freelance photographer specializing in artistic approaches.*

Super Suggestion:

♥ **Protect those pink noses.** For sensitive pink-skinned noses that might sunburn, rub in Sunblock 45 everytime they go outside.
—*Contributed by Kim Monteith of Colorado Springs, CO. Her white Arabian's pink nose is pampered every day!*

—*Photo contributed by Kendra Bond of Buzzards Bay, MA.*

Faces

Warm Winter Facial

Wipe any dust off your horse's face with a plush terry cloth hand towel. Wet the towel with warm to hot water and wring it out completely. Keep it twisted until the last minute to preserve steam and then slowly and carefully open it up flat on his face. Let it sit steaming for 5 - 10 seconds. Then, wipe around his forelock, eyes, nose and cheeks. Repeat as often as you like.

Then, take a second dry towel and gently dry his face. Rub a small amount of baby oil or lanolin around his eyes and nose to prevent chapping in cold weather.

—*Contributed by Paree Hecht of Commack, NY.*

WHOA:
Make sure the water is warm and not hot when you try the Warm Winter Facial. And, be careful when you apply the towel to your horse's face. Sudden movements might scare him.

April Jordan, a Holsteiner mare, gets a steam facial when the weather gets cold. —Photo contributed by Paree Hecht of Commack, NY.

Cool Summertime Facial

Soak a clean sponge with lukewarm water. Wipe your horse's face around his eyes, outside of his ears, muzzle and nostrils. Let the excess water drip down his face.

Optional: For a real refresher, add a dollop of a mild liniment (such as Vetrolin) to the water and rinse his face.

Mary Ellen's Corner
When I wipe liniment on Mary Ellen's face, I prefer Vetrolin. It seems to be milder than the others. I'm always careful not to get any in her eyes.

Gentle Facial Massage

Hold your fingers closely together and work them firmly, but gently, in small circles. Start in between the ears, working down to the muscles of the forehead and just over the eyes (use a very light touch over the eyes). Then, work your fingers down each cheek and massage each side of the jaw deeply. Lightly circle the eyes and ears with the tips of your fingers, and then run your fingertips repeatedly straight down his entire face. When your horse is completely relaxed, softly brush away all the hair you've loosened.

Pampered Ears

Moisten a clean sponge with warm water and wring it out completely until almost dry. Clean just inside the ear flap, wiping upward and outward to clean out any insect bite scabs, ticks, or flakes of dried skin. Do not go deep into the ear canal!

Mary Ellen's Corner
I use a sponge to clean ears, not a towel. The loose ends of a towel might flap in their eyes and spook them. Mary Ellen loves to have her ears cleaned. She pushes toward me when she understands what I am about to do!

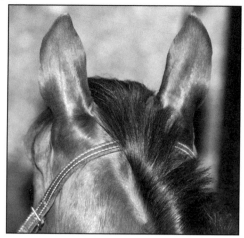

—Photo contributed by Lynette Farlow of New York, NY.

Brushing Their Teeth

You'll need a hoof dressing brush (the kind that looks like a big toothbrush). Gently, push your horse's lip up and brush up and down over his front teeth. You can brush over the gums as well. Freshen in warm water frequently. Reserve this brush for his teeth only and store it (after it is completely dry) in a plastic bag to keep it free of contamination.

—Contributed by Mary Welch of Lawrenceville, GA. Brushing Aruba Breeze's teeth, her 18-year-old Thoroughbred, makes it easier to worm him and have his teeth floated. She doesn't recommend flavoring the brush with anything. The time she tried it, Breeze tried to nibble on the brush.

Super Suggestion:

❤ **Rub 'em the right way.** Horses prefer to be rubbed, not patted. Rub horses on their head, neck and around their ears.
—Contributed by John Lyons of Parachute, CO. A famous horse trainer, John teaches his methods at sold-out seminars across the country with the help of Bright Zip, his 22-year-old Appaloosa.

A date with Dad.

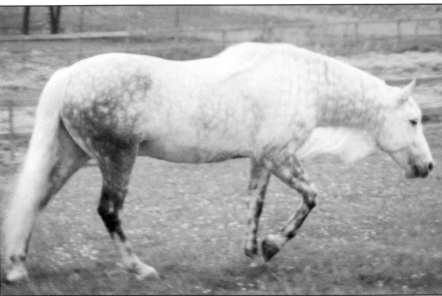

Single Tree Comanche Warrior, an adopted Mustang, has a mane that's over three feet long at its longest.
—Photo contributed by Marcia Goins of Single Tree Farm, Cross Plains, TN. This horse (and his mane!) is so fabulous we had to give him a whole page!

Mane & Tail

Mane & Tail Skin Invigoration

Materials:

    Human hair brush
    Spray on conditioner
    Mane comb
    Alcohol

First, brush the mane and tail thoroughly, following the instructions for brushing on page 18. Then, place the mane comb at the roots of the mane (directly on to the skin). Scrub out any dandruff or scruff by wriggling the comb firmly back and forth. Then, comb any flakes completely out. In this manner, you are invigorating the crest of the mane.

Next, invigorate the tail. Press the comb directly on the skin of the dock (bone of the tail) and firmly rake the comb downward. Most horses will love this, twisting their tail around to help you reach the

Dales pony stallion. —Photo contributed by Canadian Mountain & Moorland Society of Nova Scotia, Canada.

itchiest spots. Invigorate and comb the entire dock, loosening dandruff and checking for ticks.

When you've finished, brush the entire tail through to clean out dandruff and scruff. Apply alcohol (or Betadine solution) to any scabs from tick bites and spray conditioner directly on to dandruffy spots.

Author's note:
Watch out! Ticks can crawl up your horse's tail and lodge themselves right around the very end of the dock. Dab some alcohol on a tick to kill it and then remove it with tweezers. Or cover the tick with a large gob of petroleum jelly. It will suffocate and fall off, or be easily picked off with tweezers.

Super Suggestions:

♥ **Get picky.** To keep tail hair breakage to a minimum, use a human hair pick to gently separate hairs and free it of tangles. —*Contributed by Marcia Goins of Single Tree Farm, Cross Plains, TN.*

♥ **Desnag the burrs.** To remove burrs or a particularly bad tangle, spray on conditioner generously and let it dry. Then, hand separate hairs to loosen burrs or tangles. If you know your turned-out horse will get burrs caught in his tail, spray on conditioner before he even goes out. It will make it easier later to remove the burrs.

♥ **Watch out for over-conditioning.** If your horse is showing, too much conditioner will make his mane and tail too slippery to braid or band. To give the hair some stiffness and remove the conditioner, mix one quart of white vinegar in a bucket of warm water, rinse mane and tail thoroughly, and let dry.

Super Suggestions:

💗 **Join the braiding bunch.** Braiding will keep your horse's tail tangle-free and clean. Use an old bed sheet and cut it into long strips about six inches wide. Loosely braid the strips into the tail below the end of the dock. Check 2 - 3 times a week to make sure it's not rubbing. Or try a tail bag available at tack stores. —*Contributed by Mary Harwelick of Garwood, NJ.*

💗 **Add a splash for the well-groomed horse.** Splash a little Vitalis onto your hands and run them through his mane to make him smell good. —*Contributed by Jo Milliron of Reynoldsburg, OH.*

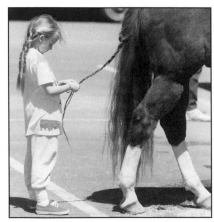

—Photo contributed by Suzanne Drnec of Hobby Horse Clothing Company, Chino, CA.

26

Mane & Tail

Deep, Down Mane & Tail Conditioning Treatment

Materials:

> 1 - 2 cups Mane 'n Tail Conditioner
> 1 - 2 cups mineral oil
> 1 tablespoon Tuttle's Elexer

Mix the ingredients together. You may need to make more, depending on the thickness and length of your horse's tail.

After the mane and tail are completely brushed and free of tangles, massage the mixture into the skin of the dock with your fingers. Keep applying conditioner and generously massage all the way to the end of the tail bone. Add an extra dollop of conditioner at the very end of the tail bone and rub in well.

Next, squeeze conditioner down from the top of the tail through the strands of hair to the ends. Generously coat the very end of the tail where hairs are the most dry. When completely coated, either let tail hang free to dry naturally or for deep, down conditioning, put it in a tail bag to soak.

While the tail is setting, start the mane. Press a thick line of conditioner into the base of the mane all along the crest, including the forelock. Work the conditioner into the roots of the hair and skin all along the crest. Treat this as an energizing massage as well. Comb extra conditioner out to the ends of the mane and forelock. Let your horse stand in its stall for 15 minutes while the conditioner soaks in. Then, shampoo and rinse out completely.

Mary Ellen's Corner
In the summer, Mary Ellen's coat suffers a bit from the sun and repeated bathings to keep her cool. I mix the above ingredients in a bucket of warm water and rinse her entire body. She soaks for 1 to 2 hours before I shampoo it off.

I always use conditioner made for horses. The human kind has too much perfume which attracts bugs!

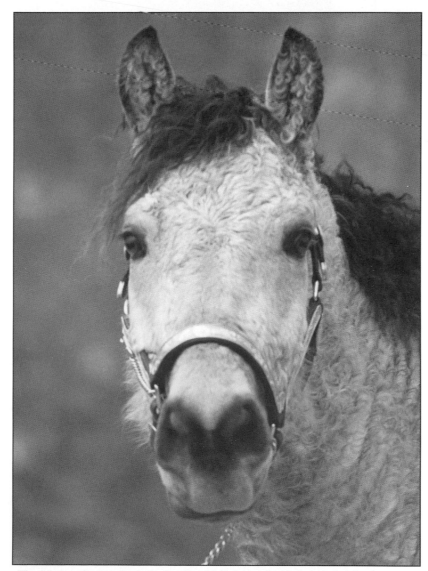

The American Bashkir Curly is a breed especially known for it's long and curly winter coat.
—Photo contributed by the American Bashkir Curly Registry of Ely, NV.

Mane & Tail

Bug & Tick Relief

Saturate the roots of the hairs with Listerine to clear up any bug or tick bites. Let dry and brush through. Or rinse the roots with a Betadine solution. Apply straight to any scabs.

—*Contributed by June Laughlin of Bedford, VA.*

Listerine Dandruff Therapy

Mix equal parts of Listerine and baby oil together in a bowl. Rub into dandruffy skin of mane or tail and rinse. For really bad dandruff, let it soak for 15 minutes and rinse well.

—*Contributed by Melinda Johnson of Coldspring, TX.*

Mary Ellen's Corner
When using Listerine, I am especially careful that the excess does not run into Mary Ellen's private parts under the tail. Place a towel under the tail while you splash on Listerine. Or pour Listerine into a clean spray bottle and mist the itchy spots.

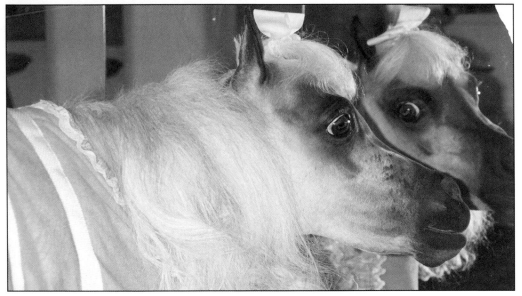

Penelope eyes herself in a mirror! —*Photo contributed by Sandy Larkin of Webster, NY. Penelope does many guest appearances, one of which was on the Maury Povich Show.*

Creamy Listerine Regime

Materials:

      1/2 cup creamy baby oil
      1/2 cup Listerine
      1/2 cup Tuttle's Elexer

Mix the ingredients together well in a bowl. Rub into the skin of the mane and tail, and squeeze excess through entire tail. Let soak for 15 minutes, shampoo out, and rinse well.

—*Contributed by Melinda Johnson of Coldspring, TX.*

End of Tail Scrubby

Find the end of the dock in your horse's tail. With a curry or mane comb, rub the end of the tail bone with the teeth to loosen scaly skin and scabs. Then, apply a small amount of Nitrofurazone to the tip of the tail and massage in.

Mary Ellen's Corner
Mary Ellen loves this. I rub for as long as she wants! You can also do this with the spray nozzle of the hose when you bathe your horse.

Sesame Oil Mane & Tail Massage

Warm sesame oil or vitamin E oil (available from health food stores) by setting the container in a bucket of warm water. Oil should be warm to the touch, not hot. Evenly coat entire mane and tail with oil, and massage deeply into the hair roots and skin. Comb extra oil to the ends of the hair. Place a tail bag on the tail and let oil stay in a few hours or overnight. Then, shampoo and rinse well.

—Contributed by Wendy Vinitsky of Agoura, CA.

Quickie Hot Oil Treatment for Tail Ends

Heat two tubes of VO5 Hot Oil Formula in a bucket of warm water. Oil should be warm to the touch, not hot. Wet tail ends with warm water and apply oil, carefully coating all ends. Leave on for 15 - 30 minutes. Then, shampoo and rinse well.

—Contributed by Melinda Johnson of Coldspring, TX.

Mary Ellen's Corner
When I use any gooey treatments on Mary Ellen's tail, I do them inside the barn. Outside, she flips her mane and tail around chasing flies, which splashes the treatment all over her body.

The Jac Be Nimble is a world champion reining horse. —Photo contributed by Lorie Shaw of Portage, PA. At first glance he looks like a miniature horse because his mane touches the ground but, The Jac Be Nimble is a full-sized Quarter Horse stallion who even has a hair-care conditioner named after him!

Lynn's Econo Detangler & Instant Fly Repeller

Mix one part Avon Skin So Soft with ten parts water. Spray onto tangles and brush out. This preparation fulfills two jobs: swishing tails detangle while the scented swatting action repels flies!

—Contributed by Lynn Borden of Middletown, NY.

Super Suggestion:

❤ **Don't fret over mudglobs.** If he has big wet globs of mud in his mane, just let them dry and then roll the clumps back and forth in your hands, crumbling the dried mud. Then brush normally. This will prevent ripping the hairs out.
—Contributed by Dawn Lyons of Lana Lobell Farms, Montgomery, NY.

Dawn Lyons and Speedy Crown at Lana Lobell farms. She says her life revolves around caring for this great sire. Speedy is lucky to have her. —Photo contributed by Gena Gallagher of Columbus, OH. Gena is the art director for Hoof beats, a publication of The United States Trotting Association.

Styling the Pampered Horse's Mane

The Alternative to Pulling a Horse's Mane

Pulling a horse's mane thins and shortens the hair, making it easier to braid and band for showing. However, if a horse is retired, turned out, ridden for pleasure, or simply hates to have his mane pulled, this trimming solution may be easier than pulling, and looks better than simply cutting it straight off. It will never have the grace of a pulled mane and most mane-pulling purists will know the mane has been cut. But it is easier and possibly more fun to do, especially if you have a hidden desire to be a hair stylist.

Everyone says horses don't feel the pulling, but I know

Mary Ellen, my 21-year-old horse, hates it. Why, I don't know. I do know my trimming procedure is much less stressful for her. Since I only ride her for pleasure, I want our relationship to be one of friends. I don't want to do anything to cause her discomfort, whatever that may be.

Her comfort comes first. See the results on page 33. It really doesn't look so bad.

1

Materials:
    Brush
    Scissors
    Mane comb
    Thinning shears

2

Brush the mane thoroughly. To separate each hair, flip the mane over to the other side of the neck and brush close to the roots to remove every tangle. Then return it to its original side and brush it flat.

Mary Ellen's Corner
Mary Ellen has a long graceful neck and looks best in a shortish mane about four inches long. Choose the best length for your horse by trimming a little at a time until you achieve the desired look.

3

With the scissors and a mane comb, separate a small piece of mane at the root near the ears. Comb it straight up (like a mohawk) and trim the ends straight across from right to left (use the regular scissors, not thinning shears).

Then, separate a second, small clump of hair adding a little of the first trimmed pieces as a guide to make sure you're cutting evenly. Again, comb it straight up and trim right to left, even with the previously trimmed pieces. Follow this procedure for the entire mane.

Repeat the procedure just to check yourself and make sure you haven't missed any long hairs. Trim only a little at a time or you may trim off too much!

Super Suggestions:

💜 **Make safety foremost.** Only use blunt end scissors to guard against accidents.

💜 **Mist for manageability.** A light misting will help hair stay in place while you trim. Spray with water, or use a solution of equal parts water and white vinegar. Don't use spray-on conditioner, as it will make the hair too slippery to grasp.

💜 **If at first you don't succeed ...** This procedure takes practice. If you are not confident about it, don't try it before a show or outing!

💜 **Don't overcut bushy manes.** Since you are only trimming and not thinning, bushier manes may clump a bit when they hang. Trim them a bit longer, so that the added weight will hold them down.

💜 **Shape long tresses if you please.** You can shape a long graceful mane by following these steps as well. Instead of trimming straight across for Steps 3 and 4, trim it into the curved shape that you wish.

Styling

4

After you have finished Step 3, stand back and look at it. You may decide to skip Step 4 (which layers the mane for a more natural look), and just go on to Step 5.

Comb the mane to the other side of the neck (the side it normally does not fall on). You may need to spray on some water to make the hair stay manageable.

With the mane laying flat on the horse's neck, separate off a small clump of hair. Trim evenly straight across from left to right. Separate and trim another small clump of hair, adding a little of the first trimmed pieces to help you line up an even cut. Continue this procedure until the entire mane is done.

5

Then, recomb the mane flat on the side of the neck that it normally lays on. Trim off any long hairs hanging down with the thinning shears. Run your fingers through the mane up from underneath to separate out any more long hairs, and trim off.

Helpful Hint:
You might need to do Step 5 again, in a week or so, to trim long hairs that were missed earlier.

The last step: Treat your patient horse to a handful of carrots and a kiss.
—Photo contributed by Gemma Giannini of Barrington, IL.

6

Trimming the Forelock

1 Comb the forelock down and trim straight across from right to left. Use blunt end scissors and be extra careful of your horse's eyes!

2 Then, standing at the side of the horse's face, recomb the forelock out to a sharp angle (see diagram). You are trying to make a slightly layered look. Too much of an angle will create too many layers and it won't look as natural. If your horse's forelock is very thick, you will need to trim it in sections like you did the mane.

Above and right—two examples of a pulled mane to compare with Mary Ellen's trimmed mane, far right. —Photos contributed by Charlene Strickland of Bosque Farms, NM.

Mary Ellen modeling her styled and trimmed mane. It doesn't look so bad! —Photo contributed by Judy Decker of Johnson, NY.

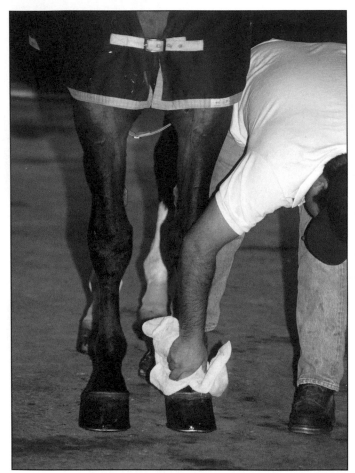

Terrific legs! —*Photo contributed by Lynette Farlow of New York, NY.*

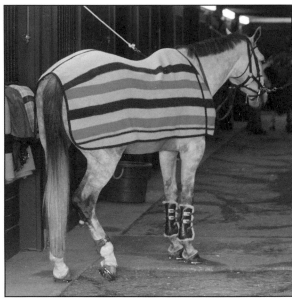

—*Photo contributed by Lynette Farlow of New York, NY.*

Hot Legs!

Simple Liniment Revitalizer

Rub on your favorite commercially prepared liniment and massage in well. Pay particular attention to any area of heat. Do not wrap immediately after rubbing legs, as you might blister sensitive horses.

Light Rub 'n Wrap

Splash on alcohol and rub lightly. Wrap with thick pillow or fleece wraps. (The thicker the wrap, the better. They contour to the leg and provide a more comfortable support.) Then, cover entire wrap with a standing bandage.

WHOA:
Racetrack grooms recommend: don't wrap unless absolutely necessary. It's easier to notice swelling from potential problems when the legs are unwrapped (then wrapping legs may be helpful). Always check with your vet or trainer on what is best for your horse. Most horses will not need the additional support of bandages.

If you're not sure how to wrap a horse's leg, have your vet or trainer show you before trying it on your own. No matter how precise book instructions are, they will never quite convey the correct feeling of how wraps should fit.

Two-Hour Listerine Sweat Refresher

Apply Listerine liberally to legs. Then, simply wrap Saran Wrap around lower leg encasing just the cannon bone (the bone below the knee and hock), tendons and ankle. Let the horse stand in the stall and eat hay. If necessary, hand graze him if he tries to pull the saran wrap off. After two hours remove the saran wrap and hose the legs with cool water.

Or, after applying Listerine, you can wrap the leg with wraps before covering it entirely with Saran Wrap. Then, secure with standing bandages to hold them in place. These can stay on overnight.

Mary Ellen's Corner
In the summer when Mary Ellen spends a couple of hours in the barn away from bugs, I put Listerine Sweats on her hind legs. Since she is a bit arthritic in her ankles, it relieves the swelling from "stocking up" when she stands for long periods of time without moving around. I remove them before she goes back outside. You can use a Listerine sweat on yourself, too. I do when my ankles hurt!

Super Suggestions:

❤ **Powder up after rubbing down.** Apply a light dusting of baby powder under leg wraps for a horse who gets rubbed. First, lightly brace the leg with witch hazel, let dry, and then apply the baby powder and wrap. —*Contributed by Jennifer Bates, barn manager of Hunterdon Farms, Pittstown, NJ.*

❤ **Bring soothing relief.** After strenuous activity, try poulticing from ankle up to and including knees or hocks. —*Contributed by Wendy Noseworthy of Bloomingburg, NY. Try the widely used Pol-Cat Poultice to soothe.*

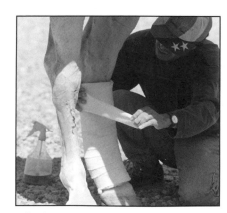

During a massage or when wrapping legs, apply liniment with a spray bottle. It's easier and less wasteful. —Contributed by Anne Kursinski of Flemington, NJ. —Photo contributed by Lynette Farlow of New York, NY.

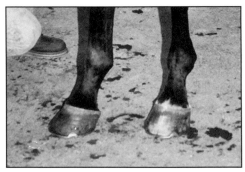

—*Photo contributed by Lynette Farlow of New York, NY.*

—*Photo contributed by the Pony of the Americas Club of Indianapolis, IN.*

Big feet or little, they are cute! —*Photo contributed by Charlene Strickland of Bosque Farms, NM.*

Pampered Hooves & Feet

Before applying any creams or packings, carefully pick out your horse's feet with a hoof pick. Then, brush loose debris out of the sole and off the hoof wall with an old stiff brush. Pick his feet daily and check for wounds and soreness.

Maximizing Moisturizing Hoof Pampering for Shelly, Shod Feet

Materials:

Tuff Stuff hoof sealer
Bear-Cat Hoof Formula

Pick out your horse's feet and brush any dirt off the hoof wall and sole (the bottom of the hoof). Paint Tuff Stuff on to the hoof wall about 1 to 1-1/2 inches from the ground up. Paint nail holes well and let dry. If your horse is unshod, pick up the foot and paint the very edge of the hoof wall that touches the ground. Do not paint the heels or the sole.

Massage the hoof cream into the the heel, hoof wall above the dried Tuff Stuff, and coronet band (the hairline area where the hoof begins).

Then, pick up a foot and press the hoof cream into the sole and frog (triangular shaped pad under the hoof). Pack enough so that it's just shy of level with horse shoe or hoof wall. This will prevent suction from sucking the packing out of the hoof when the horse walks away.

Mary Ellen's Corner
I once had a horse with incredibly healthy and hard (not dry) feet. He was trimmed regularly and it was recommended to us that he remain unshod. Even though he was shown frequently, he required nothing on his feet. In contrast, Mary Ellen must wear shoes all the time and needs all the help she can get from creams, sealers, and packing.

Super Suggestions:

- **Hands-off for hooves?** Much has been said about leaving a healthy horse's feet alone—no creams, packings, etc. Check with your farrier about your horse's feet, their condition, and what's best in your climate.

- **In with biotin.** If your horse's feet are especially shelly or crumbly, check with your vet or farrier about a biotin supplement to help your horse heal his feet from the inside.

- **Healthy feet, healthy horse.** Hooves should be trimmed and checked by a farrier every 6 - 8 weeks.

- **Work the grease without the grime!** A clean cement floor or rubber mats over a dirt floor are best when applying creams or packings to feet. If you're on a dirt floor with no mat, use a small piece of linoleum (or even plywood) under the foot as you work on it. Be careful not to drag the linoleum along the floor, as the sound might spook your horse.

Super Suggestions:

- **Don't overdo it.** In wet climates, too much hoof oil and dressing will soften the hoof. It can cause the nail holes of shod horses to give, thus loosening the shoes. If this is a problem, dispense with the dressings, or apply to the coronet band and sole only.

- **Prevent heel scratches.** Regular turnout on chilly wet mornings or even too much bathing in cool weather can cause heel scratches (chapping of the skin at the back of the pastern). To help prevent this, apply a thin layer of Nolvasan or A & D Ointment to the back of the pastern during everyday grooming. Allowing fetlock hair to grow longer during this chillier season will help keep the moisture away from the heels.

- Or try this special preventive remedy for heel scratches from George Morris: mix equal amounts of Nivea and Neosporin together and apply to heel scratches.
  —*Contributed by Jennifer Bates, barn manager of Hunterdon Farms, Pittstown, NJ.*

Pampered Hooves

Ivory Liquid Foot Bath

Add 1/4 cup of Ivory Dishwashing Liquid (or try Betadine solution or even Castile soap) to a bucket of warm water. Use a clean scrub brush and wash the underside of each foot. Carefully use a sponge to wash the outside of the hoof wall and the heel. Never scrub the hoof wall with anything abrasive. (The hoof wall is covered with a natural moisture retaining layer called the Periople which should not be removed.) Rinse the hoof well, let dry (or dry with a towel) and apply your favorite cream, if desired.

Epsom Salts Bath for Tired, Achy Feet

Add a cup of epsom salts to a large, shallow bucket or round feed tub filled with warm to hot water. Cross tie the horse and place both front feet in the bucket. Let soak 5 - 10 minutes. Most horses will stand nicely in a bucket of warm water. Dry feet with a towel.

Natural Snow Care

Turn your horse out on a snowy day. The snow will clean his feet and encourage additional blood flow to the area.

For horses who are shod, keep the snow from icing and balling up in their feet by coating the sole and shoe with petroleum jelly or PAM cooking spray. Before returning to the barn, pick out any snow or ice that may have accumulated to prevent him from slipping.

A & D Ointment Treatment & Massage

For excessive dryness, squeeze about three inches of A & D Ointment (available at grocery stores or pharmacies) onto your fingers. Apply to the entire hoof and vigorously massage it into coronet band. Pack the sole and frog with extra ointment.

Penelope in her "shoes"—bunny slippers! One winter when Penelope got sick, Sandy brought her in the house to keep her warm. There she stayed! She must wear something on her feet to keep from slipping on the wood floors. —Photo contributed by Sandy Larkin of Webster, NY.

Hoof Oil for Peanuts

Even the pros look for ways to save money when they can and here's a great example: using peanut oil instead of hoof oil for painting the coronet band, sole and frog. It's cheaper, so it's less of a problem if you spill it (which happens often enough in the excitement at a horse show). Peanut oil is available at most grocery stores.

—Contributed by Cyndi Mottolese, barn manager of Peter Leone's Lionshare Farm, Greenwich, CT.

All-Natural Bacon Grease Method

Yes, you can use bacon grease if you really want to. In warm weather, simply paint it on hooves and sole. If weather is cool, and the bacon grease has congealed, use a clean spackle knife (or your fingers, if you can stand it) to pack it into soles and frog. Immediately discard any excess to avoid attracting flies, rodents, and nasty looks from other people in the barn.

Dryness Alleviater for Arid Areas

Here's another gooey natural treatment for dry hooves. Melt one cup of lard in the microwave for 30 seconds (just until soft), mix in a teaspoon of Betadine solution, and paint the mixture on entire hoof. Or let harden and apply as a hoof packing with a clean spackle knife.

—Contributed by Beth Roberts of Gilbert, AZ.

WHOA:
Be careful melting lard in the microwave. It should be heated only until soft, not hot. Too-hot lard will burn you!

Super Suggestions:

❤ **Condition for two.** Massage human hand cream into the coronet band. It's great for the hooves and hands!
—Contributed by Kristen Schwieger of Agoura, CA.

❤ **Send dryness packing.** Pack very dry feet with a commercially prepared mud mixture available at most tack stores. Pack a small amount into the sole and place the foot down onto a piece of paper about the size of the hoof. This will hold the packing in when the horse walks away.
—Contributed by Caren Goodrich of Louisville, KY.

❤ **Give some aching relief.** Soothe soreness by packing feet with a cooling Pol-Cat poultice.

❤ **Flush the thrush.** If your horse's foot is showing signs of thrush, try flushing the foot with hydrogen peroxide. Otherwise, treat it with a commercially made preparation, such as Thrush Busters.
—Contributed by Darlene Williams of Green Valley Tack, Pine Island, NY.

39

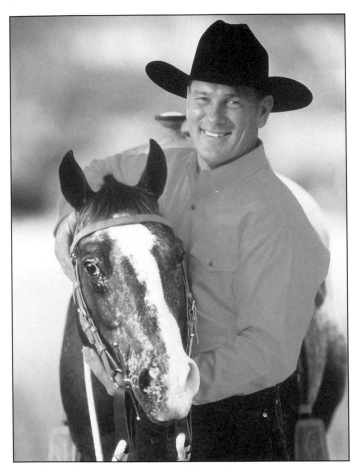

"Even if he doesn't need it, I give Zip a bath just because it makes him feel good!"—Contributed by John Lyons of Parachute, CO.
—Photo contributed by Terry Turk-Hobbs of John Lyons Symposiums, Parachute, CO.

"That little extra bit of pampering can mean the difference between first and fifth in a race."
—Contributed by Jean Bernard of Columbus, NJ. She and her husband train and race in the New York and New Jersey area.
—Photo contributed by Caren Goodrich of Louisville, KY.

Ultimate

BATHING

Super Suggestions:

- **Keep it warm.** Always use warm water. Never give a cold bath unless you are hosing down leg joints for therapeutic purposes!

- **Beat the cold water blues.** No hot running water in your barn? Try this: your hardware store should carry adaptors that let you hook up a garden hose to your kitchen sink. Attach it and run the hose out the nearest window or door.

- **Let the sun do the work.** In the morning, set out several full buckets of water in direct sunlight. By the time you are ready to bathe, the water will have been warmed by the sun.

- **Spray it again, Sam.** Use a spray nozzle attached to the end of the hose. It will help save water and your horse will enjoy the invigorating spray. Most important, a powerful spray will help remove all the soap when you rinse.

Sudsy 6-Step Bathing Beauty Basics

What could possibly feel better than a long, relaxing bath on a hot day? If you make baths as soothing and as comfortable as possible, your horse will soon look forward to them.

1

Materials:

- Hose with spray nozzle
- Buckets
- 2 sponges
- Horse shampoo
- Sweat scraper
- Towels

2

Fill both buckets with warm water and drop a sponge into each one. Add shampoo to one of the buckets and leave the other filled with just warm clean water for rinsing the horse's face later.

3

Cross-tie your horse in a wash stall. With the spray nozzle at fine to moderate pressure, start by slowly spraying a front leg nearest you to accustom him to the water. Then, work your way over the whole body until it is thoroughly wet. Do not spray his face or around the ears.

With the soapy sponge, scrub entire horse except his face. Clean under the tail and between the hind legs as well. Rub shampoo from the bottle directly onto dirty areas or stains and any white leg markings. Let soak and begin step 4.

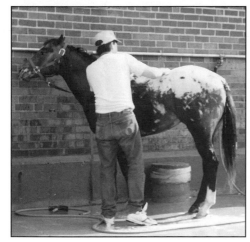

—Photo contributed by the Pony of the Americas Club, Indianapolis, IN.

4

In the meantime, pour shampoo directly on to the horse's mane and tail and scrub into the skin and roots of the hair. Squeeze excess shampoo through the ends of the hair and let soak.

5

Wring out the soapy sponge completely and carefully wash your horse's face and nostrils. Always wash his face last, to prevent soap from running down into his eyes.

6

Dampen the clean sponge you've saved and rinse his face off first. Then, rinse off the rest of the horse thoroughly with the hose. Rub your hand against his hair to test for any remaining soap. Then, use a smooth-edged sweat scraper to remove excess water. If the sweat scraper picks up any excess soap, rerinse and scrape again. Any soap left on will dull his coat and might even irritate his skin. Then, rub him well with dry towels. Let him completely dry in his stall or in a grassy field.

Mary Ellen's Corner
We don't have a wash stall and I never tie Mary Ellen when I bathe her. I just loop a long lead rope over a fence rail and hold on to it. With the lead rope attached to her, she thinks she is tied to the fence post. Should she get upset and start to pull back, I loosen the lead rope and she doesn't fight.

Super Suggestions:

❤ **Be sure the weather's balmy.** Only bathe your horse in warm weather. We recommend that you bathe your horse only when it is 75 - 80 degrees or warmer. If you'd feel uncomfortable standing there wet, then your horse probably would, too. Always cover him with a cooler(s) afterwards if it's a bit chilly.

❤ **Keep your eyes on the feet.** Horses with soft feet can suffer from daily bathing. After a bath, wipe your horse dry with a towel and pay particular attention to drying his legs, fetlocks, heels and hooves. Or try to avoid daily bathing.

—Photo contributed by Suzanne Drnec of Hobby Horse Clothing Company, Chino, CA.

- **Only the best "poo" will do.** Use the commercial brands of horse shampoo. They tend to be milder than human shampoos or dish washing liquid.

- **Get that deep down dirt.** Before bathing, rub really dirty spots such as hocks, knees, elbows and manure stains with undiluted shampoo. Let them soak while you get the water to the perfect temperature.

- **Spare the kisser.** Never put undiluted shampoo directly onto your horse's face—as it will be next to impossible to rinse out. Use a wrung-out soapy sponge to clean his face and nostrils instead.

- **Use a soft touch for thin skin.** For scrubbing thin-skinned horses and faces, try a Scrubby Bath Cloth by Epona. It's like a Handi-Wipe except with a little bit of tooth.

Ultimate Baths

Itchy Spots
Curry & Rub Bath
(for Really Dirty Horses)

Materials:

        Basic bath materials
                (see page 42)
        Rubber curry comb
        Grooming mitt
        Towel

Before bathing, curry the entire horse with a rubber curry comb to loosen all dirt. Use a grooming mitt on his face and legs.

Spray off loose dirt with warm water and shampoo the entire horse, using the rubber curry and grooming mitt to work up a lather. Be sure to keep the soap off his face. For additional scrubbing power, apply extra shampoo directly into the curry comb to scrub his hindquarters and itchy spots: belly, neck and chest.

Then, while he is still dripping wet with soapy water, bring him to his stall or someplace out of the sun. Let him soak for up to 30 minutes. He can eat hay, nap, or even roll. The soaking causes the dirt to rise to the surface and will rinse right off. Make sure he doesn't completely dry out, because dried-on soap is difficult to rinse out and might cause dandruff or skin irritations.

Once he has soaked, wash his face with a wrung-out soapy sponge and then completely rinse him off. Scrape with a sweat scraper, rub down with a towel, and let dry.

Helpful Hint:
This is a super bath for turned-out horses who tend to be dirty from rolling and gummy from fly spray. Use only milder horse shampoos since the soap remains on for up to 30 minutes. Don't use this bath on a frequently bathed horse; it will be much too drying.

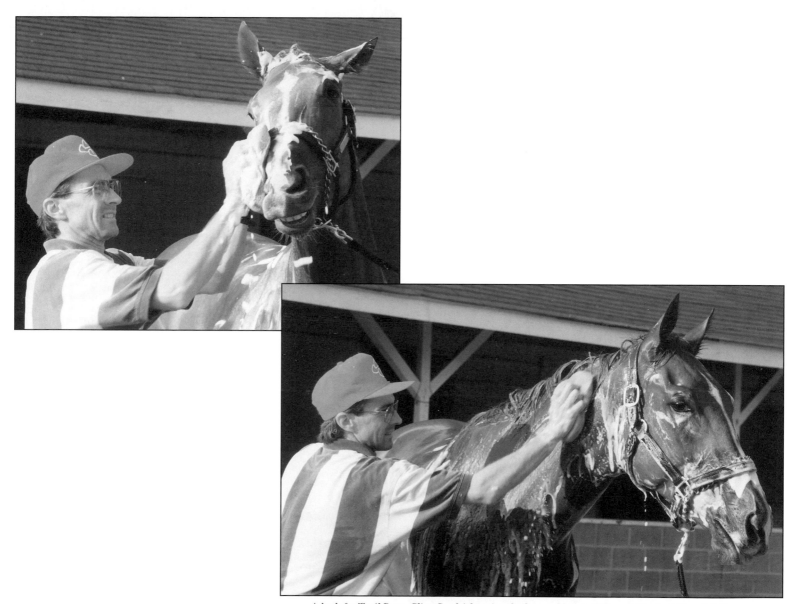

A bath for Trail Dust. Clint Goodrich trains the 2-year-old racing Thoroughbred at Churchill Downs.
—Both photos contributed by Caren Goodrich of Louisville, KY.

Super Suggestions:

❤ **Cool out with a summer misting.** On hot days, fill a spray bottle with water and mist your horse to keep him cool. Add a touch of Vetrolin liniment for a cool breeze. —*Contributed by Robin Stryker of Lititz, PA.*

❤ **Keep the breeze coming.** On scorching hot Arizona summer days, I hose Sparky off for ten minutes with warm water and put him near a fan which creates a breeze. It helps keep him comfortable and cool especially before he eats. —*Contributed by Anita Cantor of Scottsdale, AZ.*

❤ **Splash on the refreshment.** Generously soak your horse with a splash bath of liniment and water. Then, gently scrub all over with the Grooma Soft Touch Brush. —*Contributed by Becki Kempes of Pottsville, PA.*

Ultimate Baths

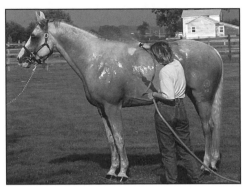

—*Photo contributed by Gemma Giannini of Barrington, IL. She is a freelance photographer whose work appears in many equestrian magazines nationwide.*

Simple Fresh Water Shower

On hot days, spray your horse thoroughly with warm water. Use a spray nozzle attachment so the water pressure is strong enough to completely clean out dirt and dried sweat. Let him drip dry in the coolness of the barn.

Mary Ellen's Corner
Mary Ellen loves to be bathed. She gets very gummy in the summer from all the fly spray and sweat, so I bathe her once a week and give her daily quickie showers during hot weeks for fast relief. A clean horse attracts less flies than a dirty one.

Deluxe Chamois Bath & Coat Conditioner

Materials:
    1 - 2 chamois cloths
    4 - 6 tablespoons baby oil
    3 cups water
    Clean spray bottle

In a clean spray bottle, mix the baby oil and water together. Set aside.

First, bathe your horse thoroughly and scrape him off well with a sweat scraper. Then, dampen a clean chamois cloth with the prepared solution (shake the solution well before each use), and rub the horse vigorously while he is still wet. As the chamois cloth becomes too wet, wring out completely and remoisten with the solution to continue. Rub down entire horse. Then, let him dry in a clean stall.

Let the chamois cloths dry out and use them later as a final rub down after each grooming. It will add a little oil to the coat.

"She just loves mud! Afterwards, I indulge her in a warm bath." —Contributed by Michelle Simpson of Claremore, OK. —Photo contributed by Charlene Strickland of Bosque Farms, NM. Charlene is an author of five equestrian books and contributing editor of over 450 articles.

Anti-Fungal Betadine Rinse

Mix 1 - 2 cups Betadine Solution in a bucket of warm water. Sponge off the entire horse liberally with solution. For scrapes or mild fungal infections, apply some Betadine at full strength, let soak, and rinse out with Betadine solution. Rinse light colored horses with plenty of water to prevent possible staining.

Helpful Hint:
An occasional Betadine bath can help prevent fungal or bacterial growths which can be caused by hot and wet weather. Always check with your vet when you notice any fungal irritation. Betadine baths can be drying, so only occasional use is recommended.

Mary Ellen's "Fave" Romp & Roll Method

Spray entire horse with warm water until he is soaking wet. Then, just turn him out in a paddock. Let him roll and graze as much as he wants. When it's time to come in, spray off the dirt with warm water and let him drip dry in a clean, deeply bedded stall. When he is dry, brush well.

WHOA:
Bathing too often can remove the natural oils from the skin, causing the coat to be dull and the skin dry. We recommend bathing only once a week or before a show. Rinse sweat off after a ride with plain water or try the Vetrolin Sponge Bath Refresher.

Vetrolin Sponge Bath Refresher

Mix one cup Vetrolin green liniment or alcohol in a bucket of warm water. Sponge off entire horse liberally. Pay special attention to the chest, neck and between the hind legs on stifling hot days. Scrape off with a sweat scraper.

—Contributed by Liz Hoskinson of New York, NY.

Mary Ellen's Corner
I gave Mary Ellen a Vetrolin bath and then sprayed her with fly spray. When I turned her out, I noticed the smell of Vetrolin helped keep the flies at bay better than just fly spray alone!

Luxurious After-Bath Finisher

While your horse is still wet from a bath, spray conditioner on his entire body, mane and tail. Then, rub his coat vigorously with a plush terry cloth towel. Don't spray his face directly. Instead, spray a little conditioner into the towel and rub his entire face.

The Wash-O-Matic method, with Ko Ko in the rinse cycle.
—Photo contributed by Lee Moody of North Augusta, SC.

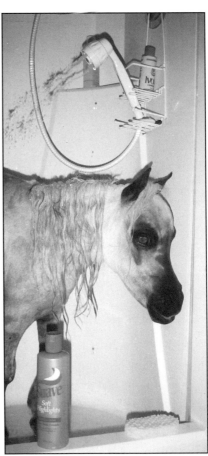

Penelope in the shower. —Photo contributed
by Sandy Larkin of Webster, NY.

Five attendants per horse and no less! Ice water cooling station in the vet box after the Kimberly
Clarke/AHSA Field Trials in 1994. —Photo contributed by Katherine Walcott of Wilsonville, AL.

Alpha Keri Rinse

Here's a great way to add a little oil to the skin of frequently bathed horses. After a bath, pour 2 - 3 capfuls of Alpha Keri Bath Oil into a bucket of warm water. Rinse entire horse. Scrape with a sweat scraper and then rub well with a terry cloth towel.

—*Contributed by Jennifer Bates, barn manager of Hunterdon Farms, Pittstown, NJ.*

Alice's Olympic Rinse Bath

Materials:

    1 capful of Avon Skin So Soft
    2 capfuls of Absorbine
        Refreshment
    1 capful of Tuttle's Elexer
    1 chamois cloth

Mix ingredients together in a bucket of warm water and rinse horse completely. Rub excess water off with a chamois cloth. Conditions the coat and keeps the bugs away, too!

—*Contributed by Alice Walls of Renton, WA. She mixed this refreshing bath for the horses who prepared for the 1996 Olympic selection trials.*

Tea Rinse

In a gallon of hot water, steep 5 - 10 tea bags. Allow the tea to cool and use it to rinse the horse completely. If you don't have hot water in your barn, put 5 - 10 tea bags in an old nylon stocking and let them steep in a gallon of water in direct sunlight. (If the tea bags break apart, the stocking will hold the leaves in so they won't spoil the water.)

Only use on a dark chestnut, brown, bay or black horse! Like a henna for humans, it will bring out the depth of color in the coat. Do not use on a light colored or grey horse, as it will stain their coat.

—*Contributed by June Laughlin of Bedford, VA.*

Super Suggestions:

♥ **Only use towels fit for a king.** When toweling the pampered horse, remember: only the plushest terry cloth towels and wash cloths will do!

♥ **Try the chamois shortcut.** Use a chamois cloth to rub down after a bath instead of a towel. It will absorb a lot of water and it shortens drying time. —*Contributed by Alice Walls of Renton, WA.*

♥ **Don't forget the itchy spots.** When toweling off your horse after a bath, be sure to pay extra attention to the areas he can't reach to scratch. He'll love it! —*Contributed by Liz Hoskinson of New York, NY.*

♥ **Chill out on winter bathing.** In the winter, the well-groomed horse will not need a bath. The oils he accumulates in his coat will help him stay warm.

—Photo contributed by Sharon Evelich of North Bergen, NJ.

Ultimate necessity?

Ultimate necessity!
Foal wearing a sweat shirt to keep warm.
—Photo contributed by Sunspot
Pintabians of Karlstad, MN.

Killarney in his Baker sheet jammies before bedtime! —Photo
contributed by Margaret Holzacher of East Hampton, NY.

22-year-old Hobie Cat and his necessities:
hat, glasses and tennis shoes!
—Photo contributed by Carol Kirshenbaum of Bridgeton, NJ.

Ultimate
NECESSITIES

❤ When taking your horse's temperature, tie a bright-colored shoelace and a clothespin to the thermometer. The clothespin lets you pin the thermometer to the tail and the shoelace's bright color will make it easy to find if it drops in the bedding.
—*Contributed by Darlene Williams of Green Valley Tack, Pine Island, NY.*

Absolutely Vital Data

✛ Normal pulse: 30 - 40 beats per minute. Normal respiration: 10 - 30 breaths per minute. Resting temperature, taken rectally: 98 - 101 degrees.

✛ Annual check-ups should include shots, a dental exam and floating (rasping) the teeth if necessary.

✛ Worm your horse every two months and rotate wormers.

✛ Shoe or trim every 6 - 8 weeks.

✛ Keep all emergency numbers by your barn phone: vet, farrier, fire, police, 911 or emergency number, parents or friends, and tack store (as knowledgeable horse people, they can help you when you can't reach your vet).

✛ Above all—in emergencies, stay calm and call your vet with the facts.

Daily Essentials

H₂0 Facts

Pampering your horse begins and ends with the most important ingredient in his life—water. A horse will drink eight to ten gallons of clear, fresh water each day. The season, time of day, how hard the horse's body is working, whether he is ill or in good health, young or old, and the state of any injuries will all affect how much more or less he drinks.

Dump out and freshen the water for stalled horses, at least once, preferably twice a day. They prefer clear, clean, lukewarm water. It has been found that horses really prefer water between 45 - 65 degrees. Ice cold water is not particularly liked by horses, even on the hottest summer days.

—*Contributed by Holly Covey of Chick's Harness & Supply, Harrington, DE. She is president of the Delaware Equine Council.*

Mary Ellen's Corner
I freshen Mary Ellen's water twice daily. She loves it fresh and will not drink it if it has been sitting even 5 - 8 hours. Since she is older (21 years old), I always make sure she receives an adequate amount of water.

Every necessity is an opportunity to pamper. —Photo contributed by Alecia Barry of West Greenwich, RI.

WHOA:
A horse, at rest, should have access to fresh water (as much as he wants) at all times. However, offering unlimited water (especially cold water) to a hot and sweaty horse can result in colic or founder. If you drank an ice cold glass of water after running a mile, you'd get a stomach ache, too—and the stomach ache a horse gets is much more severe.

Cool your horse out after exertion (by walking until cool). Allow him to drink several swallows of lukewarm water at about 10 - 15 minute intervals during the cooling out process until his respiration and temperature are back to normal.

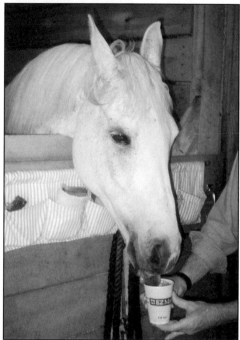

In the winter, their "afternoon tea" is buckets of warm water. Sometimes apple juice is added to the bucket as well! —Contributed by Linda Hurth of Nederland, CO. —Photo contributed by Ray and Victoria Wallick of Ellsworth, MI. Here we see Riff, their 17-year-old Arabian, lapping apple juice right out of a cup.

Winter Water Serving Tips

In the winter, most horses will tend to reduce their water intake, especially if the water is too cold. Add warm water to their water bucket to encourage them. If you don't have hot water in the barn, fill a clean milk jug or thermos with very hot water. Mix it with fresh water from the spigot and serve warm, not hot.

Horses will love the added warm water. Once a regular routine is set, your horse will immediately drink once you pour the water into his bucket. For added entice-ment, try adding a pint or so of apple juice.

Watch your horse's daily water consump-tion and alert your vet if he doesn't drink enough. Lack of water can lead to a life-threatening colic situation as well as other health problems.

Super Suggestions:

💜 **Try the peppermint trick for finicky drinkers.** If your horse is finicky about drinking water at shows, add a peppermint drop or a dash of peppermint extract to his water bucket every day, and do the same when away. It will fool a horse into drinking what tastes like the same water. *—Contributed by Holly Covey of Chicks, Harrington, DE.*

💜 **Double up for dunkers.** For horses who dunk their hay and foul up their water, fill one water bucket near his hay for dunking and another across the stall that will remain clear and fresh. *—Contributed by Holly Covey of Chicks, Harrington, DE.*

💜 **Replenish with electrolytes.** For horses who are worked hard, fill one water bucket with plain water and another with water and electrolytes (see page 58). *—Contributed by Anne Kursinski of Flemington, NJ. Anne rode for the USET in the 1996 Olympics on show jumper, Eros.*

Super Suggestions:

❤ **Keep tanks fresher easier.** Instead of a large outdoor tank, try using a smaller tank or clean garbage can. You can dump it every day and add fresh water. —*Contributed by Bonnie Lass of Godeffroy, NY.*

❤ **Clean out any debris.** An old tennis or badminton racket is handy to scoop leaves out of the outside water tank. —*Contributed by June Laughlin of Bedford, VA.*

❤ Or a plastic colander with a handle. —*Contributed by Helen Zahrndt of Spencer, SD.*

❤ Or a small fish net.—*Contributed by Rose Marie Lessa of Burney, CA.*

❤ **Warm up outside tanks, too.** In the winter, mix a kettle or two of boiling water with the ice cold water of the outdoor tank for a lukewarm cocktail. —*Contributed by Connie Berto of San Anselmo, CA. Careful not to burn yourself on the hot kettle, and <u>never</u> carry a kettle of boiling water over snow and ice! A safer alternative then is using hot tap water instead.*

Daily Essentials

Outside Tanks

Even if you have a pond or a running stream, always offer horses a tank full of water as an alternative. Place it in an open area so horses approaching to drink will not feel trapped in a corner.

Your tank should be large enough to serve your horses all day. They should never be without water outside, especially in hot weather. The tank should not be too small or lightweight that a horse can dump it over, and it should be wide enough that a horse can get his head into it without fear. There are many commercial tanks available and some even have plugs near the bottom for easy emptying. A bath tub can make an acceptable water tank, but be sure to check for any sharp edges.

"Treat each horse as an individual. Analyze what is the best possible care for that individual so he can be and perform at his best." —Contributed by Leslie Burr-Howard of Westport, CT. Pictured here: Leslie competing on Gem Twist in Palm Beach, Florida. She has been successful in the show ring for almost 20 years.—Photo contributed by James Leslie Parker of Ridgefield, CT.

Bucket Cleaning

Cleaning buckets is an important part of horse care and essential for encouraging your horse to drink water.

Rinse out buckets daily and sponge out any scum. Two to three times a week, mix a heaping tablespoon of baking soda with a cup of warm water and scrub the bucket with a brush or sponge, before rinsing thoroughly and refilling.

Once a week, thoroughly clean both water and feed buckets. Squirt a dash of Ivory Liquid into the buckets and fill to the brim with warm water. Let them soak if necessary (especially to loosen up caked-on gunk around the edge of feed buckets). Scrub out with a brush or sponge and rinse repeatedly until completely soap-free.

"We use white feed and water buckets so you can tell when they are absolutely and completely clean." —Contributed by George Morris of Hunterdon Farms, Pittstown, NJ. In the equestrian business for 50 years, George is one of the most respected and influential people in the industry. —Photo contributed by Lynette Farlow of New York, NY.

Cleaning Tanks

Be sure to include outside tanks in your bucket cleaning routine. Pick out any floating debris daily and replace the water every 2 - 3 days. Scrub tanks with baking soda or Ivory Liquid once a week and rinse thoroughly.

WHOA:
When using soap to clean anything that will hold drinking water, always rinse it thoroughly! Horses will not eat or drink from anything that smells of soap.

Super Suggestions:

♥ **How clean?** Scrub your water buckets so clean that you can drink out of them yourself! —*Contributed by Jennifer Volker of The Standardbred Retirement Foundation, Blairstown, NJ.*

♥ **Scrub and refresh.** Clean water buckets with a toilet brush and add a dash of minty mouthwash to freshen them up. —*Contributed by June Laughlin of Bedford, VA. Buy a new toilet brush for this purpose only. (Never use an old, used toilet brush on your horse buckets. Yuck!)*

♥ **Eliminate "new plastic" odors.** Some horses will not drink from buckets smelling of plastic. If that's the case, soak new water buckets overnight with a dash of vinegar and rinse thoroughly to get rid of that plastic smell. —*Contributed by Holly Covey of Chicks, Harrington, DE.*

♥ **Watch the clock.** Most horses are bothered by interruptions to their routine. Keep them as stress-free as possible by feeding at the same times each day. *—Contributed by Carol Maxwell of Johnson, VT.*

♥ **Put on the "frequent feeder" miles.** Feed smaller meals more often during the day, instead of one or two big meals. Your horse will love the extra "mealtimes" and will look forward to getting the royal treatment from you. *—Contributed by Joyce Aurich of Draper, UT.*

—Photo contributed by Charlene Strickland of Bosque Farms, NM.

Daily Essentials

Feed Facts

Along with water, fresh hay and feed are essential to keeping a healthy, happy horse. Good quality hay and grass are the most important part of a horse's diet. They help aid in the digestion of grains, keep him warm in winter, and keep him entertained and full. Grain is supplemented if hay and turnout can't meet the horse's energy requirements. Check with your vet on what's best for your horse.

Examine all feed carefully before you serve it. Good lighting in your hay storage area and feed room will help you inspect hay and feed for mold. Hay should have a greenish color throughout and the bale should smell fresh. An unpleasant musty odor indicates mold even if you can't see the telltale black and white signs.

Feed, too, can get moldy. Look closely at the grains and check for any greenish or white discoloration. Moldy feed (especially corn) or hay can cause a horse to severely colic or even founder.

Store grain in clean garbage cans or metal lined feed bins to keep rats and moisture out. Garbage cans are easier to handle when dumping out older grain and filling with new. Store all feed in a room that can lock out a loose horse. Horses who overeat grain can colic or founder.

Feed horses in smooth-edged buckets attached at shoulder height. Throw away any leftover feed—if left behind, it can get rancid and attract flies.

Mary Ellen's Corner
1150-pound Delta, an easy keeper, requires only a handful of feed daily. 1075-pound Mary Ellen, on the other hand, needs 5 pounds of feed and supplements daily. Both are in their early 20s and retired. They are turned out on 10 acres of pasture for 12 - 20 hours daily and, when inside their stalls, are given hay free choice (as much as they want).

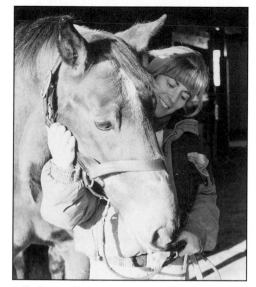

"I always add warm water to Speedy Crown's feed to soften it. He looks forward to it."
—Contributed by Dawn Lyons of Montgomery, NY.
—Photo contributed by Judy Decker of Johnson, NY.

Hats Off To Bunny, a Standardbred racehorse, awaiting her Slop 'n Slurp. —Photo contributed by Sharon Evelich of North Bergen, NJ.

Slop 'n Slurp Delight

You can also always add water to your horse's feed. Add warm water in the winter and cool water in the summer. Pour in enough so it's level with the top of the grain. Some horses may not like it too watery, so experiment with your horse to see what he likes best. It's a great way to sneak additional water into their diet!

—Contributed by Nanci Falley, the American Indian Horse Registry of Lockhart, TX. Remember, serve the water warm or cool, not hot or ice cold!

Mary Ellen's Corner
Mary Ellen really loves this. I've fed her food with water since she turned 20. I can slip in her nasty-tasting supplements and once in a while, a crushed-up Bute. She laps it all up! Although it presents a special bucket cleaning challenge, it's well worth it when she is happily slurping away.

In other barns, the sound at feed time is crunching. Ours is lapping and slurping. It's such a happy, contented sound!

Super Suggestions:

♥ **Know his measurements.** Invest in a height and weight tape. Knowing your horse's precise measurements is the key to feeding him properly. *—Contributed by Darlene Williams of Green Valley Tack, Pine Island, NY.*

♥ **Don't just scoop it, weigh it.** About "a half scoop" of feed doesn't tell you that your horse is receiving the correct amount for his size. Always weigh it for accuracy. *—Contributed by Darlene Williams of Green Valley Tack, Pine Island, NY. The "Scale Scoop" has a scale built right into the feed scoop. Just scoop it up and it tells you the weight.*

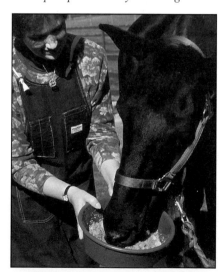

—Photo contributed by Gemma Giannini of Barrington, IL.

Super Suggestions:

❤ **Keep the block clean as a lick.** Keep the salt block clean. Every now and then, scrub all the gunk off. — *Contributed by Rose Marie Lessa of Burney, CA.*

❤ **Make it easier for the old guys.** Buy salt in the loose form for older horses. They may have trouble scraping the blocks with their teeth. Set it out in a bucket in a sheltered area so they can help themselves. —*Contributed by Rose Marie Lessa of Burney, CA.*

❤ **Share your salty favorites with a friend.** Try salted pretzels as treats. Horses love them, and they're a great source of additional salt. —*Contributed by Orlando Fasano of Centereach, NY.*

❤ **Put the brakes on speedy eaters.** For a horse who bolts his feed (eats too fast), place a salt block in his feed bucket. It will slow him down by forcing him to pick around it. —*Contributed by Darlene Williams of Green Valley Tack, Pine Island, NY.*

Daily Essentials
Accessible Salt

Salt with trace minerals added (red colored) is recommended, since some hays or grains may be deficient in the minerals that this kind of salt provides. Keep a small block in a salt block holder in the stall and one large block in the pasture, to allow free access to salt any time your horse needs it.

The Ol' Salt-in-the-Bucket Trick

Or, attach a small "special treats" bucket to the wall inside the stall and keep a layer of loose salt at the bottom. When you serve treats in this bucket, you'll sneak a little extra salt into your horse when he licks them up. For extra punch, drop in a wet carrot! And, for active horses, mix in 1 to 2 ounces of electrolytes for every hour of hard work.

WHOA:
Electrolytes are only recommended for horses who exert themselves through competing or racing. They help restore salt and potassium afterwards like Gatorade does to humans. Electrolytes should not be fed to an idle horse. Your vet should advise you if and when your horse needs them.

If you are serving the electrolyte cookies at right, resist the temptation to overfeed! Just a few will do!

Electrolyte Recipe

Ingredients:

   1-1/2 cups lite salt
   2 cups table salt
   1 roll of Tums (calcium carbonate)

—*Contributed by Dr. Sarah Ralston of New Brunswick, NJ.*

Electrolyte Nibbles

Ingredients:

   7-1/2 cups sweet feed
   3 cups molasses
   1/2 cup water
   1 cup electrolytes
   2-1/2 cups of flour

Preheat oven to 350 degrees. Grease mini-muffin tins and set aside. Mix sweet feed, molasses and water together, adding electrolytes and flour slowly to create a sticky mixture. Add more or less flour as needed. Press a small amount of the mixture into each muffin tin. Bake for 20 minutes or until dark brown. The resulting cookie will be a hard treat that can easily be carried with you.

—*Contributed by Eileen Cornwell of Jupitor, FL and Jolee Brunton of San Diego, CA. Eileen adapted Jolee's recipe to sneak electrolytes into her endurance horse. Just a few cookies will do!*

Cooking for Your Horse? Of Course!

To Mash or Not to Mash?

Much has been written lately about the pros and cons of bran mashes. We've checked with our vet and she's given us the go-ahead to serve them. It is our recommendation that you check with your vet about your own horse. In any case, should you choose to mash, these recipes will entice any horse.

Mashes can be fed about once a week. If you do feed them more often, you will need to add a calcium supplement. But again, check with your vet.

Don't save uneaten mashes for later. Always clean out the feed bucket and throw the leftover portion away. Mashes can ferment and make a horse sick.

The bran itself needs to be checked for freshness, as well. If you pick up a handful, it should sift cleanly out of your hand. If the bran flakes hold together with a cobweb-like dust, then it should be discarded.

Quick 'n Easy Bran Mash

Ingredients:
>   4 - 5 cups feed
>   4 - 5 cups bran
>   Warm water

Combine ingredients together in a feed bucket, adding water to make the mash like oatmeal. Serve warm, not hot.

Sweet & Soupy Bran Mash

Ingredients:
>   4 - 5 cups feed
>   4 - 5 cups bran
>   1 cup molasses
>   1/2 cup brown sugar
>   Warm water

Combine ingredients in feed bucket and add enough water to make it the consistency of pea soup. Serve warm, not hot.

Super Suggestions:

♥ **Water up for the after-mash.** Make sure there is plenty of fresh water available when feeding a bran mash. Most horses will drink quite a bit afterwards.

♥ **Keep fruit and veggie treats fresh.** In the summer, keep a cooler in your car or in the barn for your carrots and apples so they can be served cool. (In the winter, it helps keep the fruit from freezing.) —*Contributed by Patricia Noonan of Naperville, IL.*

♥ **Nuke 'em a winter warmer-upper.** For a warm winter treat, warm (don't cook) a carrot slightly in the microwave before bringing it out to the barn. It's a great warm appetizer—but make sure it's cool enough to eat! —*Contributed by Connie Berto of San Anselmo, CA*

♥ Or simply soak carrots in warm water and serve! —*Contributed by Sara Tradewell of Warwick, NY.*

Early morning at Del Mar Thoroughbred Club racetrack in Del Mar, CA.
—Photo contributed by A. Toward.

Mmmm! —Photo contributed by Julie Krone.
Julie's friend, Stefanie Freundlich, takes over the
reins and pampers Julie's 27-year-old Filly, who is
still showing successfully.

Yummy stuff. —Photo contributed by Julie Krone. Julie has had Filly, a Shetland cross, for 20 years.
She says most of all her days are now spent with Thoroughbreds, but she remembers back
to the best days which were spent with her pony.

Cooking for Your Horse!

Julie Krone's "Filly" Filling Mash

Ingredients:

    2 cups regular feed
    5 cups bran
    1 apple, quartered
    3 carrots, cut in halves
    1 tablespoon sugar
    Warm water

Mix all ingredients and add hot water until all ingredients are moist. Serve warm, not hot.

—*Contributed by Julie Krone, one of America's leading Thoroughbred jockeys and the only woman jockey ever to win the Belmont Stakes.*

WHOA:
Any adjustments to your horse's diet should always be checked with your vet. Remember to feed a bran mash warm or cool, not hot!

Afternoon Tea Mash

Ingredients:

    4 cups bran
    3 cups oats or regular feed
    2 carrots, chopped
    1 apple, chopped
    1 regular tea bag
    2 chamomile tea bags
    Water

In a feed bucket, combine all ingredients except tea bags and water. Set aside.

In a separate container, steep tea bags in 1/2 gallon of hot water for 2 - 3 minutes. When ready, throw tea bags away and mix water with ingredients in feed bucket. Add more hot water if necessary. Let soak for five minutes and serve warm.

—*Contributed by Jennifer Snyder of Hidden Hills, CA.*

WHOA:
It was brought to our attention by our vet that caffeine from tea or chocolate will possibly cause a positive on a urine test. Be aware of this and use caution at horse shows.

Light Raisin Mash

Ingredients:

    Regular serving feed
    1 cup bran
    1/4 cup raisins
    Warm water

Combine dry ingredients together in a feed bucket. Add enough water to make it as liquid as pea soup. Serve warm, not hot.

Moxie's "Italian Style" Bran Mash

Ingredients:

    1 cup bran
    1 clove garlic, crushed
    Warm water

Mix enough warm water with bran and garlic to make it slightly soupy. Mix it right in with his dinner or feed it separately afterwards.

—*Contributed by Bernice Duguay of New Brunswick, Canada. Her horse, Moxie, has a cow bell outside her stall that she has learned to ring for service. She rings it and the equally well-trained Bernice responds.*

A Little Something Extra for Your Older Horse

Legend, a 30-year-old school horse, recently retired from Claremont Stables in New York City (yes, New York!). —Photo contributed by Claremont Stables of New York, NY.

25-year-old Misteyna with friends. —Photo contributed by Phyllis Hubbard of Corydon, IN.

"Up 'n Bucking" Senior Mash

Ingredients:

    6 - 8 cups bran
    2 carrots, grated
    2 apples, finely chopped
    4 tablespoons salt
    1 cup molasses
    1/2 cup brown sugar
    Warm water

In a feed bucket, dilute the salt, molasses and brown sugar in 3 - 4 cups hot water until it dissolves. Add the bran, carrots, apple and mix well. Add more hot water to make mash the consistency of pea soup. Serve warm.

Mary Ellen's Corner
21-year-old Mary Ellen loves this recipe! I use less water as she prefers it thick like oatmeal. Always provide plenty of fresh water for them to drink after their mash. And, remember, mash only once a week. More frequently and you will need to add a calcium supplement.

Smooth & Sweet Pellet Dinner

Ingredients:

    Regular serving of pelleted feed
    1/2 cup molasses
    1 cup sweet feed
    1/4 cup corn oil
    Warm water

Mix ingredients together and add warm water until it is level with the top of the feed. It's a great way to sneak in daily vitamins and supplements.

—Contributed by Claire Fox of North Highlands, CA.

Mary Ellen's Corner
I sneak Mary Ellen's supplements in by just adding 2 - 3 cups warm or cool water to her meal. I use Equine Senior feed which dissolves rather quickly. The dinner becomes mushy and the supplements, mixed in, are well hidden.

Macintosh Mash

Ingredients:

    1 Macintosh apple
    1/2 cup sweet feed

Grate apple directly into a feed bucket and mix in sweet feed. Serve immediately or the apples will ferment!

Chiquita's Mashed Veggies

Boil fresh carrots or green beans until they're mushy. Serve warm, not hot.

—*Contributed by Hallie McMorrow McEvoy of Hinesburg, VT. Hallie, a licensed AHSA judge, bought Chiquita when she was in her 30's (yes, she bought her) to get her out of the terrible situation she was in.*

Oat 'n Peels

Ingredients:

> 1 carrot
> 1/2 cup whole oats or feed

Shred a carrot with a potato peeler. Mix peels with oats directly into bucket. Serve immediately or the carrot peels will ferment.

—*Contributed by Jennifer Rosin of Alberta, Canada*

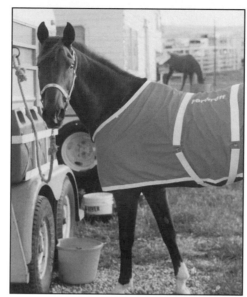

22-year-old Wraff, an endurance horse, has completed over 6,000 miles of competition and is still actively competing. —Photo contributed by Dianna Chapek of Marysville, CA.

Carrot Pâté Sandwich

Ingredients:

> 5 carrots, diced
> 1 sprig of parsley
> 1 slice wheat bread

Boil carrots until soft and mash into a paste. Spread on a piece of soft wheat bread, add a sprig of parsley and serve warm, not hot.

—*Contributed by Dinah Shamash of Ontario, Canada.*

Super Suggestions:

♥ **Won't take their medicine? Fool 'em with flavor.** To help older horse take their supplements and medications, crush up several peppermints and mix them thoroughly with bad tasting supplements or crushed-up medications. Serve on top of grain.—*Contributed by Meagan Galinger of Valrico, FL.*

♥ Or mix supplements or crushed pills well with apple flavored gelatin. —*Contributed by Mary Kensler of Horse 'N Around Tack, Sewell, NJ.*

♥ Or mix in one tablespoon dry cherry gelatin and two tablespoons sugar.

♥ Or mix one cup of the sweetest and most molasses-filled sweet feed you can find with the supplements in a large cup or bowl. Be sure to coat <u>all</u> grains. Feed this before graining or right on top of feed. Although it seems to work with supplements, this may not work as well with really bitter medications.

63

Older Horse

Dr. Ralston's Porridge

Ingredients:

    1 pound Alfa-Maize (Bio Cubes)

    1 gallon water

Add warm or cool water to the Alfa-Maize and let it sit until fully dissolved. Stir ingredients and serve.

—Contributed by Dr. Sarah Ralston of Cook College - Department of Animal Science, Rutgers University, New Brunswick, NJ. Alfa-Maize is a brand of cube that can be bought at feed stores. It is made from alfalfa and the whole corn plant ground up together. Dr. Ralston says, "I use this instead of bran mashes and add carrots, grain, supplements— anything to satisfy!"

"Please Ma, can I have some more?"
Mary Ellen loves her mashes mushy.

Alfalfa Cube "Matzoh Ball" Soup

Ingredients:

    6 - 8 alfalfa cubes

    1/2 cup sweet feed

    1/4 cup molasses

    1 tablespoon salt

    3 tablespoons corn oil

    2 - 3 cups warm water

Combine ingredients and serve. For old horses with problem teeth, allow the alfalfa cubes to completely dissolve.

—Contributed by Lisa Bermack of The Tack Shelter, Colts Neck, NJ.

Sparky's Special Winter Bran Mash

Ingredients:

    4 cups bran

    2 cups hay cubes

    1 cup Cheerios, Corn Chex or

        Quaker Oat mix

    2 apples, quartered

    3 carrots, diced

    1 jar baby food

        (pears, apricots or

        peaches)

    Warm water

Mix ingredients together in a feed bucket. Add enough water to make it the consistency of oatmeal and serve warm.

—Contributed by Liz Merrill of Cape Porpoise, ME. Her 24-year old Sparky loves this mash!

WHOA:
We recommend that you ask your vet whether your older horse should receive a bran mash or not. Always make sure it's warm and not too hot for your horse!

Pocket Cheer!

What do horses love? A pocketful of ...

1) **Fig Newtons and Snickers!**
   —*Contributed by John Lyons of Parachute, Co.*

2) **Life Savers.** —*Contributed by Kendy Allen of Manheim, PA. She owns Misty II, a daughter of Misty of Chincoteague.*

3) **Crispix cereal and green grapes.**
   —*Contributed by Jessica McCormick of Fond du Lac, WI.*

4) **Bagels!** —*Contributed by Pam Farrior of Broad Axe Horse Supplies, Ambler, PA.*

5) **Captain Crunch.**
   —*Contributed by Cyndi Mottolese of Lionshare Farm, Greenwich, CT.*

6) **Blueberry Poptarts without frosting.**
   —*Contributed by Amy Tetervin of Pennington, NJ.*

7) **Peppermint Starlight candies.**
   —*Contributed by Alecia Barry of West Greenwich, RI. I like a treat that gives her fresh breath!*

You know your horse is pampered when he's dressed better and eats better than you do! —Contributed by Andrea Schwarting of Lowville, NY. —Photo contributed by Ray and Victoria Wallick of Ellsworth, MI.

8) **Granola Bars.** —*Contributed by Resa Webber of Oakfield Farm, Center Point, TX. They are really handy at horse shows!*

9) **Watermelon.** —*Contributed by Mary Jane Ciraco of Morning Mist Farm, Deland, FL. (Well, it won't fit in your pocket, but your horse might love it nevertheless.)*

Always Coca-Cola—Duke must have a sip! —Contributed by David Sanders of Alta, IA.

10) **Cornbread and biscuits.** —*Contributed by Lisa Collins of West Hamlin, WV.*

11) **Nutter Butter Cookies.** —*Contributed by Mariah Jacobs of Albany, VT.*

12) **Candy canes.** —*Contributed by Sally Herring of Montpelier, VT.*

13) **Skittles and peanut butter sandwiches.** —*Contributed by Becki Kempes of Pottsville, PA.*

14) **Sliced cantalope.** —*Contributed by Jennifer Buckley of Orangevale, CA.*

15) **Chips Ahoy cookies.** —*Contributed by Bonnie Kreitler of Fairfield, CT.*

16) **A sip of my Coke right out of the can!**
   —*Contributed by David Sanders of Alta, IA.*

WHOA:
The above suggestions should only be served as an occasional treat, and in small quantities! Again, caffeine (Coca-Cola) and chocolate will possibly cause a positive on a urine test, so use caution at horse shows.

"I pamper my horse with treats made from The Original Book of Horse Treats." —Contributed by Terry Redding of Summit, NJ. —Photo contributed by Pam Farrior of Broad Axe Horse Supplies, Ambler, PA.

—Photo contributed by Suzanne Drnec of Hobby Horse Clothing Company, Chino, CA.

Fawn and Boot Scootin'. —Photo contributed by Jolene Venables of Jolene's Horse Rescue, Canoga Park, CA.

Buddy 'n me. —Photo contributed by Monica Keller of Bedford, TX.

Ultimate

MENUS

—*Photo contributed by Laurie Fogus of Calimesa, CA.*

—*Photo contributed by Suzanne Drnec of Hobby Horse*
Clothing Company, Chino, CA.

Yum, yum! —Photo contributed
by Marcy Gamester of Westford, MA.

Favors & Treats

Twisted Apple Peel Party Favors

Ingredients:

    Peels from 3 apples
    6 carrots
    Green carrot top
    Confectionery sugar

Peel apples very carefully to get at least two long peels from each apple. Wrap the peels around the carrots like a candy cane. Use a toothpick to hold the peels in place temporarily. Then, tie a long piece of green carrot top (or parsley) around each end of the carrot to keep the peels in place and remove the toothpicks. Dust with sugar and serve immediately.

Sweet Potato Finger Sandwiches

Ingredients:

    1 carrot, grated
    1 apple, chopped
    1/2 cup whole oats
    1/4 cup molasses
    1 sweet potato, sliced
    1/4 thick

Mix ingredients, except sweet potato, in a bowl. (Mixture should be thick, add a dash of bran to thicken it, if necessary.) Spread a thick layer of mixture onto a slice of sweet potato and serve. Or cover with another slice of sweet potato to make a sandwich. Dribble a little molasses over the top to garnish, and sprinkle with four to five oats. Serve immediately.

—*Contributed by Lauren Schone of Bloomingdale, IL.*

WHOA:
Remember, treats should only be fed occasionally. Most important: always ask your vet whether treats are an appropriate addition to your horse's diet.

Super Suggestions:

- ❤ **Liven up the party.** Make these "party favors" right at a party as part of the entertainment. But, remember, treats made with grated apple or carrot should be fed immediately so that they don't ferment.

- ❤ **Don't skimp on service.** Arrange treats on a decorative platter and butler them to deserving horses (or owners) who may just pick off a treat!

Serving on a silver platter, nothing less will do! —Photo contributed by Margaret Holzacker of East Hampton, NY. Even VP's knuckle under to every beck and call. Margaret's husband Bob, a Vice President of News America/FSI, can't resist but give Killarney the royal treatment.

69

Favors & Treats

Bundled Carrot Twigs

Ingredients:

>   Carrots
>   Green carrot tops

Cut carrots in half, four inches long, and then cut lengthwise into very thin strips. Bundle 8 - 10 strips of carrot and then tie them together with a piece of green carrot top.

Carrot Raisin Sticks

Ingredients:

>   Molasses
>   2 carrots, halved
>   Raisins

Pour molasses into a bowl. Dip pieces of carrot into molasses and coat completely. Stick raisins to the carrots and serve.

—*Contributed by Lauren Schone of Bloomingdale, IL.*

Rabi's Peanut Butter Treats

Ingredients:

>   1 carrot, diced
>   Peanut butter

Spread peanut butter over the top of the carrot pieces and serve.

—*Contributed by Tiffany Magnett of Lexington, KY.*

Delicate Garlic Crouton Surprise

Ingredients:

>   1 cup sweet feed
>   1/2 cup corn flakes
>   1/2 cup garlic croutons
>   1/4 cup molasses
>   1 tablespoon brown sugar
>   1/4 cup corn oil
>   1 teaspoon salt
>   1 teaspoon cinnamon
>   1 clove of garlic

Fold ingredients together and serve immediately. Top with a clove of crushed garlic.

—*Contributed by Laura Loving of Loving, TX.*

Tempting Carrot Hors(e) d'Oeuvres

Ingredients:

>   White or wheat bread
>   1 carrot, diced
>   Honey

Cut sliced bread into one inch squares. Arrange squares of bread onto a serving platter and place a piece of carrot on each. Add a dollop of honey to top it off.

—*Contributed by Bronwyn Welch of Holly Hill, SC.*

Carrot Maple Tidbits

Ingredients:

>   Maple syrup
>   Bran
>   2 carrots, halved

Pour maple syrup in a bowl and on a separate plate, spread out the bran. Dip carrots into maple syrup and then roll them in bran until covered.

—*Contributed by Kim Parkes of Lake Elizabeth, CA.*

Sugared Apples

Ingredients:

> 1 apple, quartered
> 1/2 cup confectionery sugar

Pour sugar onto a plate and roll the apples in it until they're fully covered. Serve fresh before the apple turns brown.

Sugar Molasses Apples

Ingredients:

> 1 apple, quartered
> 1/2 cup molasses
> Sugar

Dip apples into molasses until coated and arrange on a plate. Sprinkle sugar on top and serve.

—*Contributed by Lelia Heidel and Tiffany Henkel of Great Falls, VA.*

WHOA:
Wherever we mention making or serving a treat on a plate, use a hard plastic plate that won't break if you drop it.

Lady and Surefire know something good is coming! —Photo contributed by April Aberle of Colmesneil, TX.

Granny's Favorite Apples

Ingredients:

> 1 Granny Smith apple, quartered
> 1/2 cup sugar
> 1 tablespoon honey
> 1 cup seedless grapes
> 1/2 cup raisins

Pour sugar on a plate and roll each apple in it until fully covered. Place in a feed bucket and dribble honey over. Garnish with grapes and raisins.

—*Contributed by Kate Baker of Palm Beach, FL.*

Snazzy Jetta Doll (Sissy). —Photo contributed by Eileen Mestas of Rancho de Caballos, Boone, CO.

Favors & Treats

Candied Apples

Ingredients:

    Molasses
    Sweet feed
    Confectionery sugar
    2 apples

Pour a thin layer each of molasses, sweet feed and confectionery sugar into three separate shallow bowls.

Either use the apple whole or cut it in halves. Roll in molasses until fully covered, then in the sweet feed, and lastly in confectionery sugar.

—Contributed by Kim Cassidy of Middletown, NJ.

Apple Crocks

Ingredients:

    1 large apple, halved
    1 lettuce leaf
    1/2 carrot, chopped
    1 small celery stalk, chopped
    1/2 cup molasses

Scrape out each apple half to make a bowl, and press a lettuce leaf into each one. Pinch off any excess lettuce leaf.

Mix the carrot, celery, and molasses together. Then, stuff the mixture into the prepared apples. Garnish with a layer of thinly diced carrots.

—Contributed by Kristine Brockman of Vesper, WI.

Sweet Stuffed Apples

Ingredients:

    1 apple
    Molasses
    1/2 carrot, grated

Core the apple like you would a pumpkin and save the top piece for later (it will be used as a lid). Then, pour molasses into the apple until almost full and sprinkle with grated carrot. Cover with apple top and serve immediately.

—Contributed by Astrid Werner of Princeton, NJ.

Sweeter Stuffed Apples

Ingredients:

    1 apple
    1/2 cup sweet feed
    1 tablespoon molasses

Core the apple like you would a pumpkin. Fill the hole with sweet feed and dribble molasses over the top.

—Contributed by Jessye Crowe-Rothstein of Lincoln, MA.

Glazed Hay Knots

Ingredients:

    Hay

    Molasses

    1 tablespoon salted and shelled
        sunflower seeds

Pick out 5 - 10 long strands of timothy from a flake of hay. Straighten them as best as possible and tie in a knot. Place directly in a feed bucket and dribble molasses over it. Garnish with a sprinkle of sunflower seeds.

Peaches 'n Bran

Ingredients:

    4 cups bran

    2 peaches, quartered

    1/3 cup sugar

    3 cups water

    Wafer cone dishes, available
        at ice cream stores

    Sprinkles

Fold all ingredients together and scoop the mixture into wafer cone dishes. Top with sprinkles.

—*Contributed by Chelsey Solomon of Parker, CO.*

Granola Snacks

Ingredients:

    1/2 cup sweet feed

    1 carrot, chopped

    1 apple, chopped

    1 cup granola or oatmeal

    Molasses

Pour sweet feed onto a plate and set aside. In a separate bowl, fold carrots, apples and granola or oatmeal together. Add enough molasses to give mixture a stiff consistency. Roll the mixture into balls about two inches wide and then cover them with sweet feed. Arrange balls on a plate or tray and sprinkle on the left-over sweet feed as a garnish. Serve immediately.

—*Contributed by Andrea Cashman of Nova Scotia, Canada.*

Form the granola balls with an ice cream scoop, or use a plastic sandwich bag as a glove to form them with your hand.

—*Contributed by Helen Evers of Goshen, NY.*

Tantalizing Tidbits

Ingredients:

    1/2 cup molasses

    1 cup whole oats or cracked corn

    2 apples, quartered

    3 carrots, diced

Preheat oven to 350 degrees. Lightly grease cookie sheet and set aside.

Pour molasses into a bowl and spread oats, or cracked corn, out on a plate. Dip pieces of apple and carrot into the molasses to coat entire piece and then roll them in the oats or cracked corn. Place them on the cookie sheet and bake until warm. Let cool and serve.

—*Contributed by Tammy Goydich of Warwick, NY.*

Super Suggestions:

- **Prepare foods "family style."** Make salads and soups in one large bucket, then, divide it into the smaller buckets for each horse to eat from.

- **Keep off the mowed lawn.** When creating salads, never use grass cuttings from a mower! They ferment and cause colic. If you are serving a salad with grass that you have cut by hand, serve it immediately before it even has a chance to wilt!

- **Don't feed them fertilizer by mistake.** Never use grass that has been recently fertilized. Wait 3 - 4 weeks and make sure there has been at least one rainfall.

"Any four leaf clover I find, she gets."
—Contributed by Teri Shaw of Ashland, OH.

Lite Fare

Canadian Cuke Salad

Ingredients:
    1 carrot, diced
    1 apple, quartered
    1/2 cucumber, sliced
    1 tablespoon sugar

Toss together carrot, apple, and cucumber in a feed bucket. Sprinkle sugar on top and serve immediately.

—Contributed by Tasha Kozushka of Manitoba, Canada.

Animal Cracker Salad

Ingredients:
    1 apple, quartered
    1 carrot, diced
    5 sugar cubes
    10 animal crackers

Toss everything together and serve immediately.

—Contributed by Carrie Landis of Harrisburg, PA.

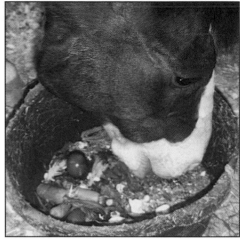

Tequilla eating her "ensalada." —Photo contributed by Terri Howard of Timonium, MD.

Tequilla's Ensalada Verde

Ingredients:
    1 carrot, diced
    5 lettuce leaves, broken
        into bite-size pieces
    1/2 cucumber, sliced
    1 radish, diced
    1 stalk celery, diced
    3 pieces cauliflower
    Corn oil

Toss all vegetables together in a feed bucket and add a bit of corn oil for a delicate flavor.

—Contributed by Terri Howard of Timonium, MD.

Spring Tonic

Ingredients:

- 1 cup alfalfa
- 1 cup red clover
- Handful of dandelions

In the early spring, clip fresh alfalfa, red clover, and dandelions from a field. Serve immediately before they wilt.

—*Contributed by Bayla Schauer of Sturgeon Bay, WI.*

WHOA:
Remember when serving clipped grass, serve it immediately and very fresh. Never serve grass clippings from a lawn mower. They can cause colic!

Alfalfa Bloom Salad

Ingredients:

- 1 cup alfalfa blooms
- 1 carrot, diced
- 1 apple, quartered

Shake out a flake of alfalfa hay on to an empty feed bag. Scoop up the blooms that fall out into a measuring cup. Mix ingredients together and serve. Make sure the blooms have freshly fallen out of the hay. Don't use old blooms off a dirty floor!

—*Contributed by Fonda Hawks of Glasgow, KY.*

Mix 'n Munch Fruit & Vegetable Salad

Ingredients:

- 1 carrot, diced
- 1 apple, quartered
- 10 - 15 red seedless grapes
- 1 slice watermelon, cubed
- 1/4 cup raisins
- 1/2 sweet potato, sliced
- 1/2 cup sweet feed
- 1/2 cup whole oats
- 1/2 cup molasses

Toss all ingredients together in feed buckets and serve immediately.

—*Contributed by Lauren Schone of Bloomingdale, IL.*

Consommé

Ingredients:

- 2 cups warm water
- 1 carrot, diced
- 5 croutons
- 1 tablespoon bran
- 1 tablespoon sweet feed

Mix ingredients together and serve warm.

Summer Gazpacho

Ingredients:

- Handful fresh grass
- Handful fresh clover
- 1/2 cup baby carrots
- 1/4 cup bran
- 1/2 - 1 cup water

Handpick the choicest pieces of grass and clover. Add carrots and bran, toss well. Add water and serve immediately.

—*Contributed by Dinah Shamash of Ontario, Canada. Remember to serve it very fresh.*

Alfalfa Bisque

Ingredients:

- 5 - 6 alfalfa cubes
- 1 - 2 cups warm water

Mix ingredients together in feed bucket, let the alfalfa cubes dissolve, and serve.

—*Contributed by Dottie Burdette of New Port Richey, FL. When it snowed one winter in Florida, Dottie kept her ponies on her back porch. They watched her and her family inside the house through the sliding glass doors.*

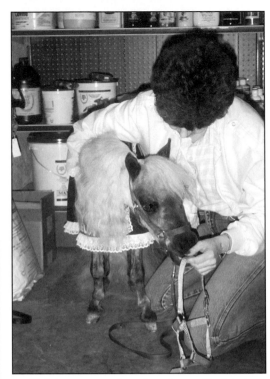

Birthdays mean a trip to the tack store. Penelope is always welcome in her tack store.
—Photo contributed by Sandy Larkin of Webster, NY.

Buttercup's first birthday. —Photo contributed by Udell and Lynn Ingles of Sorento, IL.

One year old! Mirage taste-tests a birthday cake. —Photo contributed by Michelle Simpson of Claremore, OK.

Birthday Treats

Carrot Cake

Ingredients:

> 1 cup sugar
> 1 cup light brown sugar
> 1 cup flour
> 1 cup bran
> 1 teaspoon baking powder
> 1 teaspoon baking soda
> 1 teaspoon cinnamon
> 3 cups carrots, grated
> 1-1/2 cups corn oil
> 4 eggs
> 2 teaspoons vanilla
> 1 macintosh apple, cut in sixths

Preheat oven to 325 degrees and grease a 13 x 9 inch baking pan.

In a separate bowl, mix dry ingredients and then add carrots, oil, eggs and vanilla. Beat until there are no lumps. Pour into prepared baking pans and bake about one hour. Remove from pan when cool. Garnish with apple slices sprinkled with brown sugar. Serve cool.

Bonny Birthday Apples

Ingredients:

> 1 apple
> 5 purple grapes
> 1 teaspoon brown sugar
> 1 teaspoon bran
> 1 carrot, grated
> Colorful sprinkles

Cut apple in half, scoop out center and put the pulp in a bowl. Add grapes, brown sugar, and bran, mix well. Stuff the apples with the mixture. Top with grated carrot and sprinkles as a garnish.

—*Contributed by Anne Bounds of Berlin, MD.*

Hay Bale Birthday Surprise

Ingredients:

> 1 bale of hay
> 4 - 5 cups of feed
> 5 carrots

Place a bale of hay on its side, so the rough edge is up. Wedge it against the side of the stall or paddock fence so it's supported on at least two sides. Don't cut the twine or wire from the bale just yet.

Pour the grain over the top so it trickles down into the hay. Stick carrots upright into the hay like candles. Then, cut the baling twine or wire and very carefully pull it off, trying not to topple carrots.

—*Contributed by Roni Becker of El Mirage, CA.*

Helpful Hints:
This is a super treat for a turned out horse. He can pick through the bale, move around, and come back to it. If there is more than one horse turned out, make sure you split the bale. Serve as many Birthday Surprises as there are horses turned out or they may fight over it.

If you are worried about your horse picking up too much dirt by eating small pieces of grain off the ground, substitute grain with alfalfa cubes, commercial horse treats, or baked horse cookies from page 89 - 91.

Birthday Treats

Dream's Birthday Bundt

Ingredients:

    6 cups sweet feed

    2 cups bran

    2 cups oatmeal

    1 cup molasses

    3/4 cup applesauce

    1 cup carrots, grated

    Warm water

    1 apple, sliced

Preheat oven to 350 degrees and grease a bundt cake pan. In a large bowl, mix ingredients together (except the apple). Add enough water to make the mixture doughy. Then, press the batter into the pan and bake for one hour. Flip over carefully onto a serving platter. Garnish with sliced apples, cut and serve.

—*Contributed by Christine Wegner of Wheaton, IL.*

Quick 'n Easy Bran Mash Pie

Ingredients:

    Graham cracker pie crust

    2 cups bran

    Water

    1/2 cup granola

    Apples, sliced

    Carrots, sliced

Mix bran and enough water to make it the consistency of hamburger. Scoop it into pie crust and smooth out. Top with granola, apples, carrots as a garnish and serve to several horses!

—*Contributed by Sherri Marcuccio of Litchfield, CT.*

Baked Sweet Feed Cake

Ingredients:

    2 - 3 cups sweet feed

    2 - 3 cups bran

    1/2 cup flour

    2 apples, chopped

    2 carrots, chopped

    1/4 cup brown sugar

    3 cups molasses

    1/2 cup water

    Peppermints

Preheat oven to 300 degrees. Grease a 13 x 9 inch cake pan and set aside.

Mix ingredients together, and add more bran if necessary to give mixture a stiff consistency. Spread out into a cake pan and cook for 25 - 30 minutes. Immediately top with peppermints, allowing the heat of the cake to melt them. Serve cool.

Mary Ellen's Corner
Mary Ellen really loves this cake. It makes the house smell so nice when it's cooking, especially in the winter around the holidays!

Flake O' Hay Layer Cake

Ingredients:

- 3 flakes of hay
- 2 yellow apples, quartered
- 5 carrots, diced
- 2 green apples, quartered
- 1 alfalfa cube

Place one flake of hay flat on the floor of the stall or pasture, and then place a layer of yellow apples directly on the flake. Cover with another flake and top with carrots. Cover with the last flake and spread remaining apples out on top. Garnish with a single alfalfa cube for a touch O' Green of the Irish.

—Contributed by Susie Johnson of Nags 'n Rags, Lexington, KY.

Arlene's Carrot Mold

Ingredients:

- 1 package orange Jello
- 2 pounds carrots, grated

Follow the recipe on the Jello package and add carrots. Let the jello set in the refrigerator and serve!

—Excerpted from Horseman's Yankee Pedlar of North Oxford, MA.

Cake Frosting

Ingredients:

- 2 cups bran
- 1 cup molasses
- 1/2 cup warm water
- Peppermints
- Sugar cubes

Mix bran, molasses and water together. Add more molasses or water as needed to make frosting thick and gooey. Thickly spread onto the cake. Decorate with peppermints and sugar cubes.

—Contributed by Gina Miller of Santa Cruz, CA.

Birthday Punch

Ingredients:

- 1 quart any flavor Hawaiian Punch
- 1 water bucket

Pour Hawaiian Punch (or even a tasty flavor of Gatorade) into a water bucket and fill it to the top with cool water. Leave the bucket in a communal spot for horses to sip from.

Cool Summer Mousse

Ingredients:

- 1 cup Cool Whip
- 1 carrot, shredded
- 1 apple, chopped
- Green carrot top

Fold ingredients together and pour directly into a feed bucket. Top with a bit of green carrot top. Also makes a great cake or muffin frosting!

—Contributed by Marcy Gamester of Westford, MA. She named her Morab, Moon Unit.

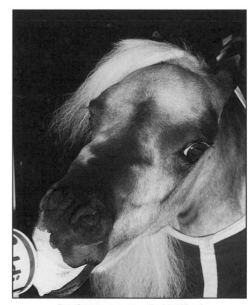

Penelope taste-testing Reddi-Whip!
—Photo contributed by Sandy Larkin of Webster, NY.

Bungee Jumper. —Photo contributed by
Robin Jason of Tack on Wheels Store,
Winston-Salem, NC.

—Photo contributed by Gaye Huettner of Cal Gaye Ranch, Paso Robles, CA.
The telephone directory lists Cal Gaye Ranch as the home of fat, happy horses.
They specialize in breeding black Arabians.

"What can I say—I love my horse! When I get a horse,
it's for life. They are never sold." —Contributed by
Sherri Marcuccio of Litchfiled, CT.

Be My Valentine Treats

—*Contributed by Dr. Sarah Ralston of New Brunswick, NJ.*

Valentine Cake

Ingredients:

    5 carrots, grated
    1 - 2 apples, grated
    1/2 cup sugar

Mix all ingredients together and mold into a heart shape on a flat plate. Cool in the refrigerator for twenty minutes and serve immediately.

—*Contributed by Carleigh Woods of British Columbia, Canada.*

I Love You Salad

Ingredients:

    1 Granny Smith apple, quartered
    1 Macintosh apple, quartered
    1 Golden Delicious apple,
        quartered
    1 Red Delicious apple, quartered
    2 carrots, diced
    1 pear, quartered
    1 tablespoon brown sugar

Toss fruits and vegetables together and sprinkle brown sugar on top before serving. Serves 2 - 4 horses. If you are only serving one horse, just use one apple instead of four. Mix it as an appetizer or top off their regular ration of feed.

—*Contributed by Ashley Hammond of Ontario, Canada.*

Cherry Mold à la Mary Ellen

Ingredients:

    1 package cherry Jello
    1 apple
    Heart-shaped baking tin
        or Jello mold
    Confectionery sugar

Follow the recipe on the Jello package and pour into a heart-shaped mold. Then, slice the apple horizontally so that you have round, flat pieces of apple 1/2 inch thick. Lay them in the jello and let it set. To serve, scoop out sections of jello and sprinkle on a dash of confectionery sugar.

Apple Heart Toppers

Slice apples horizontally, then trim off the excess to make heart-shaped apple slices. Use as a garnish or just serve!

—*Contributed by Clare Cobb of Ontario, Canada.*

CoCo has an unusual blacked-out diamond on his forehead. Looks like a Christmas ornament. —Photo contributed by Fonda Hawks of Glasgow, KY.

"I never set a price limit on Rusty's gifts. If I thought I could afford it, she got it!" —Contributed by Teri Shaw of Ashland, OH.

Stockings hung by the fireplace with care. One for Dandy, Rizz, Gamey, Pherzella, Whiskers, Rebel, Sam, Bird, Michael, and NoNo. —Photo contributed by Jam TePoel of Tazewell, VA.

Festive Holiday Menus

Peppermint Stick Bran Mash

Ingredients:

    1 cup crushed candy canes
    3 - 5 cups bran
    1 tablespoon salt
    1 carrot, diced
    1 apple, sliced
    1/2 cup molasses
    2 cups sweet feed

Dissolve crushed candy in 2 - 3 cups boiling water and let water cool to warm. Then, mix all ingredients together except sweet feed in a feed bucket. Add more warm water to make it soupy rather than crumbly. Cover with towel and let stand until cool. Right before serving, spread a thin layer of sweet feed over the top and sprinkle on a crushed candy cane to garnish.

—Contributed by Nicole Fritzler of Dryden, MI

Kristin's Christmas Horse Brownies

Ingredients:

    2 cups corn meal
    3 cups sweet feed
    1 cup bran
    1 cup flour
    2 teaspoons salt
    2 eggs
    1 cup molasses
    1/3 cup water
    3 carrots

Preheat oven to 350 degrees. Generously grease a cake pan and set aside.

In a large bowl, mix corn meal, two cups of the sweet feed, bran, flour and salt. In a separate bowl, mix eggs, molasses, and water, and then fold into dry mixture. Mix thoroughly.

Peel carrots into thin strips with a potato peeler. What you can't peel, cut into small

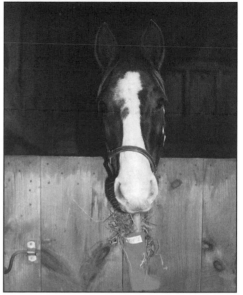

"They deserve every bit of loving treatment they get."
—Contributed by Patricia Noonan of Naperville, IL.
—Photo contributed by Jody Phillips of Hollis, NH. Here we see her horse, Laramie, with his Christmas stocking.

bits and add to mixture. The mixture will be very heavy and somewhat dry.

Press dough into the cake pan. Sprinkle remaining cup of sweet feed on top and press lightly into dough. Bake for 25 - 30 minutes. Let cool for five minutes, and then cut into cubes. Let it cool completely and serve!

—Contributed by Horseman's Yankee Pedlar of North Oxford, MA.

Festive Holiday Menus

Christmas Cake

Ingredients:

    4 cups sweet feed
    1 apple, chopped
    1 cup raisins
    1/2 cup molasses
    2 eggs
    Purple grapes
    2 carrots, diced
    Sugar cubes

Preheat oven to 350 degrees. Generously grease a cake pan and set aside.

Mix sweet feed, apple, raisins, molasses and eggs together well. Press into cake pan and bake for one hour. Remove and let cool completely. Top with grapes, carrots and sugar cubes.

—*Contributed by Edie Larson of Fox Haven Farm, Maidens, VA and The Complete Horse Tack Shop, Richmond, VA.*

Applesauce Bundt avec Corn Oil

Ingredients:

    2 cups sweet feed
    2 cups bran
    1 cup molasses
    1 cup apples, chopped
    1/2 cup applesauce
    1/2 cup corn oil
    1-1/2 cups water
    1 alfalfa cube, crushed

Preheat oven to 350 degrees. Grease a bundt cake pan and set aside.

Mix ingredients (except alfalfa cube) together in a large bowl. Slowly add more or less water until mixture is a stiff consistency. Press mixture into a bundt cake pan and bake for one hour. When cooled completely, dribble an additional 1/2 cup of corn oil over the top and sprinkle on the crushed alfalfa cube for a garnish. Remove, let cool completely and serve to several horses.

—*Contributed by Tammy Goydich of Warwick, NY.*

Apple & Carrot Pie

Ingredients:

    Corn oil
    Sugar
    4 apples
    4 carrots, diced
    Cinnamon

Pour enough corn oil in the bottom of a pie pan to cover the bottom. Then, spread about 1/4 cup of sugar over entire bottom. Slice apples horizontally in pieces about 1/2 inch thick. Lay them and the carrots down over the sugar. Pour a little more corn oil over pie and sprinkle about 1/4 cup sugar evenly over the entire top. Lightly sprinkle with cinnamon. Use a large serving spoon to serve equal portions to several horses.

—*Contributed by Kelly Carlson of Eau Claire, WI.*

Cooked Apple & Carrot Pie

Preheat oven to 300 degrees. Follow the directions above, but spray the pie pan with cooking spray before pouring corn oil on the bottom. After sprinkling with cinnamon, bake until warm and serve when cool.

"Holidays should be spent with your horse. It's nice if your family can be there, too."
—Contributed by Patrcia Noonan of Naperville, Il. —Photo contributed by Lisa Miller of Corrales, NM.

"Our pet, Mr. Magic Bars Mirage, bedecked and dazzling for the holidays."—Photo contributed by Michelle Simpson of Claremore, OK.

Shaker Boy. —Photo contributed by Marcy Gamester of Westford, MA.

Sudanna.—Photo contributed by Kathy Weymouth of South China, ME.

Serving draft horses requires a big trayful.
—Photo contributed by Lisa Miller of Corrales, NM.

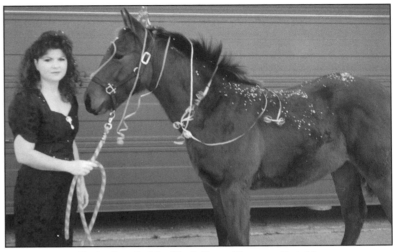

Festive dress for New Year's Eve.—Photo contributed by
Michelle Simpson of Claremore, OK.

Legend taste-testing a homemade cake shaped like a horse head.
—Photo contributed by Debbie McLeod of The Book Tree, Lenexa, KS.

Rover. —Photo contributed by
Layne Daily of Tucson, AZ.

Festive Holiday Menus

New Year's Eve Horsey Champagne

Ingredients:

    1/2 cup ginger ale
    1/2 cup warm water
    1 teaspoon sugar
    1 sprig parsley, chopped
    1 apple, quartered (optional)

Mix ingredients together in your horse's feed bucket. Top with parsley and sliced apple.

For serving several horses, borrow an inexpensive punch bowl with a dipper. Make the "champagne" directly in the punch bowl and dip out one cup per horse directly into their feed buckets on New Year's Eve.

Carrot Pâté Stuffing with Apple

Ingredients:

    1 large apple
    1/2 cup sugar
    1 carrot, chopped
    Parsley
    Purple grape

Slice the apple in half, then scoop out each center like you would a melon. Set the pulp aside.

Pour sugar onto a plate. Slightly moisten the outside of the apples. Roll them in the sugar to completely coat them and set aside.

Then, finely chop the pulp from the apple. Mix with the carrot, add a sprinkling of sugar and stuff this mixture into the scooped out section of apple. For panâche, top with a sprig of parsley and a purple grape.

—*Contributed by Anne Bound of Berlin, MD.*

Fruit Cup Supreme

Ingredients:

    1 apple, quartered
    1 pear, quartered
    1 cup Trix, Cheerios
        or Sugar Pops

Toss well and serve.

—*Contributed by Linda Singleterry of Paramount, CA.*

El Burrito Esplondido

Ingredients:

    1 soft burrito
    1 carrot, sliced lengthwise
        into four pieces
    Carrot green tops
    1/2 cup bran
    1/2 cup molasses

Lay a burrito down flat on to a plate. Put carrots side by side right on top, add a few carrot greens and set aside.

In a bowl, mix bran and molasses together. Pour mixture on top of carrots and roll burrito tightly. Wrap a green carrot top around burrito to tie it closed.

—*Contributed by Jill Fitzpatrick of The Tack Shelter, Colts Neck, NJ.*

Festive Holiday Menus

Frosty Apples

Ingredients:

        1/2 cup confectionery sugar
        1/2 cup molasses
        1 apple, halved
        2 green grapes
        Red and green sprinkles

Mix confectionery sugar and molasses together to make a thick paste. Spread it thickly on halved apple pieces. Top with green grapes and add sprinkles.

Steamed Apple Pudding

Ingredients:

        4 cups bran
        2 apples, quartered
        Water
        Cinnamon

In a large pot, combine all ingredients with enough water to make a soupy mash. Simmer on low - medium heat until the apples are mushy. Remove from stove, cover and let cool. Serve warm. Sprinkle lightly with cinnamon.

Rebel's Marinated Pears

Ingredients:

        4 cups orange juice
        2 pears
        1 cup sweet feed
        1 apple, chopped
        1/2 banana, sliced
        3/4 cup of molasses
        2 lettuce leaves
        1 carrot, shredded
        2 carrot top greens, chopped

Peel the skin off the pears with a potato peeler and cut out the core. Pour orange juice into a large bowl and submerge pears until they're covered, adding juice if neccssary. Marinate in the refrigerator overnight.

Ambition. —Photo contributed by Alecia Barry of West Greenwich, RI.

When ready, remove them from the refrigerator. In a separate bowl, mix sweet feed, apple, banana and molasses together. Then, stuff pears with the mixture and arrange on a plate decorated with the lettuce leaves. Dribble extra molasses down the sides of the pears. Garnish with a sprinkle of prepared carrot and green tops.

—Contributed by Ramsey and JoAnn Anderson of Blue Hills Lippitt Morgans, Exeland, WI.

Easy Picnicking Recipes

Muffins and cookies are great for picnics! They're easily stored in a saddle bag and can be served without utensils. And muffins are always a good treat for older horses with problem teeth.

Chancey's Bran Muffins

Ingredients:

- 1 cup flour
- 1 cup bran
- 1 tablespoon baking powder
- 1/4 teaspoon salt
- 1/4 cup vegetable shortening
- 1/4 cup brown sugar
- 1/4 cup molasses
- 2/3 cup milk
- 1 egg
- 1 carrot, grated finely
- 1 apple, grated finely
- 1 cup oatmeal

Preheat oven to 400 degrees and generously grease muffin tins. Set aside.

In a bowl, blend dry ingredients except oatmeal and set aside. In a separate bowl, beat shortening and brown sugar until light and fluffy. Then, stir in molasses, milk, and egg. Gradually add dry mixture until ingredients are moistened. Then, fold in carrots and apples. Add enough oatmeal to make batter a stiff consistency.

Scoop into muffin tins and bake 15 - 18 minutes until a toothpick comes out clean. Let cool and serve.

—*Contributed by Martha Servey of Maynard, MA.*

Itty, Bitty, Picnic Party Muffins

Ingredients:

- 3 cups sweet feed
- 1-1/2 cups molasses
- 1/3 cup water
- 1 cup flour

Preheat oven to 350 degrees. Generously grease muffin tins and set aside. Use the tiny muffin tins for making bite-sized, itty-bitty muffins.

Mix sweet feed, molasses, and water together. Add flour gradually, mixing constantly. Add flour to make batter a stiff consistency. Spoon dough into tins and bake for 15 - 20 minutes or until they are a dark brown. Let cool and serve.

—*Contributed by Aimee LaPlante of Bridgeport, NY.*

Easy Picnicking

Apple Spice Muffins

Ingredients:

    1 cup flour
    1 cup wheat germ
    1/2 teaspoon cinnamon
    1/2 cup sugar
    1/2 teaspoon salt
    3 teaspoons baking powder
    1 egg
    2/3 cup milk
    1/4 cup corn oil
    1 cup Macintosh apples,
        chopped

Preheat oven to 400 degrees. Grease muffin tins and set aside.

In a large bowl, mix dry ingredients together and set aside. In a separate bowl, mix the remaining ingredients thoroughly including the apples. Then, pour the liquid ingredients into the dry ingredients. Mix until everything is moistened. Scoop into muffin tins and bake 15 - 25 minutes. Serve cool to horses and warm to people!

Sparky's Trix & Kix Mix

Ingredients:

    1/2 cup Trix cereal
    1/2 cup Kix cereal
    1 carrot, diced

Mix ingredients together and serve immediately.

—*Contributed by Anita Cantor of Scottsdale, AZ.*

Sweet Feed Yummies

Ingredients:

    4 - 5 cups sweet feed
    3 cups molasses
    1/2 cup flour
    2 apples, grated
    2 carrots, grated
    1/4 cup brown sugar
    Confectionery sugar

Preheat oven to 400 degrees. Mix all ingredients together in a large bowl, except confectionery sugar. Form into 1-1/2 inch balls and press flat onto a greased cookie sheet. Bake 15 - 30 minutes. Let cool and sprinkle with confectionery sugar.

—*Contributed by Kristian Burns of Lafayette, CA.*

Jack's Cookies

Ingredients:

    1 cup carrot, grated
    1 apple, grated
    2 tablespoons corn oil
    1/4 cup molasses
    1 teaspoon salt
    1 cup rolled oats
    1 cup flour

Preheat oven to 350 degrees. Lightly grease a cookie sheet and set aside.

In a large bowl, mix carrot, apple, corn oil, and molasses together. Then, fold in salt, oats, and flour until mixed well. Spread dough out in one big piece on a cookie sheet. Score dough with a knife to make it easier to break apart after baking. Cook for 20 minutes or until brown. Let cool, break apart and serve.

Or try rolling dough out, cutting shapes with cookie cutters, and then baking. Great for stocking stuffers!

—*Contributed by Valerie Moore of Derby, VT. After one year of ownership, she has not stopped pampering Jack, her Quarter Horse.*

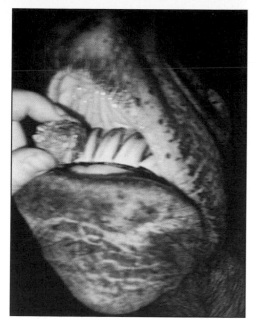

Space alien? Sea monster? No, it's just Delta taste-testing a cookie. —Photo contributed by Charles Evers of Hoboken, NJ.

Charlotte's Easy No-Cook Snaps

Ingredients:

    4 cups bran

    4 cups applesauce

Mix ingredients together. Batter should be doughy. Roll out with a rolling pin and cut shapes with cookie cutters. Let dough dry and serve.

—Contributed by Charlotte Upchurch of Fieldstone Park, Mansfield, TX.

Sweet Bran Cookies

Ingredients:

    2-1/2 cups sweet feed

    2-1/2 cups bran

    3 - 4 cups molasses

    1/2 cup flour

    2 apples, grated

    2 carrots, grated

    1/4 cup brown sugar

    Confectionery sugar

Preheat oven to 400 degrees, lightly grease a cookie sheet and set aside.

Mix all ingredients together except confectionery sugar. Mixture should have a stiff consistency, so add more flour or molasses as needed. Roll into 1-1/2 inch balls and press flat onto cookie sheet. Bake 25 - 30 minutes and let cool. Sprinkle confectionery sugar on each and serve.

—Contributed by Kristian Burns of Lafayette, CA.

Super Suggestion:

❤ **Keep your oven its cleanest.** Bake cookies in mini-muffin tins instead of using a cookie sheet. They save clean up time if the cookies are a bit too runny!

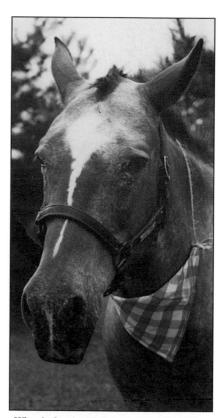

Where's the picnic? Delta is especially pert in her red-checked napkin. —Photo contributed by Judy Decker of Johnson, NY.

"We bought a farm so we could keep Rebel right at our house and give him the ultimate pampering and attention." —Contributed by Rosemary Speake of Blue Haven Farm, West Milton, OH. —Photo contributed by Suzanne Drnec of Hobby Horse Clothing Company, Chino, CA.

—Photo contributed by Suzanne Drnec of Hobby Horse Clothing Company, Chino, CA.

Draper at home. —Photo contributed by Dee Wiet of Naperville, IL.

Brand new stable for Gingersnap and Starlight. —Photo contributed by The Page family of Newton, NH.

Ultimate
STALL & STABLE

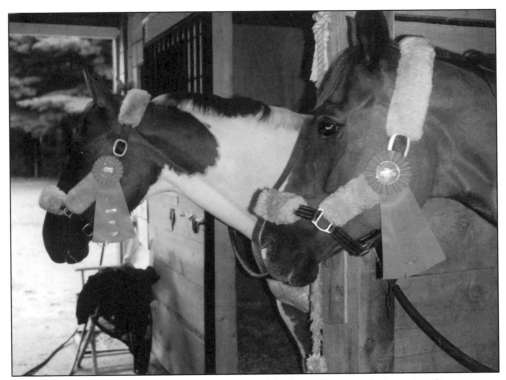

"When we built our new barn, I waited until Christmas Eve to put the horses in it."
—Contributed by Fay Seltzer of Happy Trails Western Wear & Horse Supplies, Leesport, PA.
—Photo contributed by Eileen Ricci of Fox Modular Homes, Bethlehem, CT.

Blueprint for the Utopian Stall & Stable

Here's our wish list for the ultimate in stall and stable features that deliver comfort, convenience, and safety!

1) A 12 x 12 foot or larger box stall.

2) 4 to 4-1/2 foot wide stall doors—wide enough for any horse to get through without scraping his hips.

3) Sliding stall doors, which are never in the way when left open.

4) Horse-proof latches on all stall doors and paddocks.

5) Brass name plates on the stall door (hung over a brass halter bracket, naturally).

6) Rubber or web stall guards so you can keep the stall door open for better ventilation.

7) Matching buckets for feed and water. (Optimally, buckets and stall guard should also match.)

8) Hot and cold water spigot right outside your horse's stall, so changing and adding water is easy.

9) Chest high stall walls that are solid to the ground, so a horse won't get his legs caught underneath when lying down.

10) See-through partitions (either chain link or vertical galvanized bars), between stalls above the wooden sides. Lets horses see each other and allows better ventilation.

11) No chain link or bars in the front of the stall, so horses can hang their heads into the aisle.

12) Wooden floors or cement stall floors covered with thick, rubber matts. Easier on their legs and feet.

13) Large stall windows that open upward (to reduce drafts) and can be removed in the summer.

Super Stall Situations:

❤ **Luxury.** My horse, McClaurey, has his own two-room suite. We knocked down a wall between two stalls and made one large stall which leads out to a paddock. In the summer, the door to the paddock is left open all the time. —*Contributed by Sam Savitt of North Salem, NY. Sam, a world-renowned equestrian artist, still mucks McClaurey's stall himself. He says he is a fuss-budget about it and it gives him a break from the studio.*

❤ **Deluxe.** Our horses each have a 12 x 12 box stall with adjoining 16 x 20 paddocks. The horses can go in an out freely. —*Contributed by Leslie Webb of Bakersfield, CA. Leslie was a silver medalist in dressage at the Pan American Games, riding Hannabal.*

❤ **Dream house!** Looking for a dream home where your horse can live with you? Fox Modular Homes of Bethlehem, CT has created a House/Stable combo that brings the house and the barn together under the same roof for super convenience!

Super Suggestions:

- ❤ **Keep the air circulating.** The best stable is one that is well ventilated but without drafts! A stuffy or drafty barn can cause respiratory illnesses.

- ❤ **Replace the glass for safety.** Protect your horse from any glass windows by replacing the glass with plexiglass, or by installing bars or a wire mesh grill.

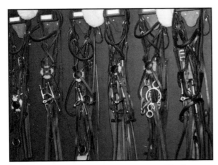

—Photo contributed by Lynette Farlow of New York, NY.

"The ultimate pampering—we bought our horses a ranch." —Contributed by Judith Sperling of JMS Products, McNeal, AZ. Buckley and Jake live on a 120-acre ranch.

Utopian Stall & Stable

14) A dutch door that opens directly from the stall to a private paddock outside. Great for ventilation and free access outside.

15) An aisle between the rows of stalls that is 12 - 15 feet wide.

16) An aisle floor that is cement, easier to sweep.

17) High enough ceilings so horses will never bump their heads.

18) Electricity and working lamps that are out of reach of curious horses, and light bulbs covered by wire protectors.

19) A 12 x 12 wash stall with hot and cold running water, overhead heat lamps, and a drain that never clogs.

20) A 12 x 12 grooming stall, or a well-lit area where you can cross tie your horse with enough room and quiet for grooming.

21) Shelves lining the grooming stall to hold every brush, cream, and oil needed.

22) A 12 x 12 feed room with a door to keep loose horses out.

23) Feed that is always delivered by someone else, directly into your feed room.

24) A heated tack room to warm yourself in the winter.

25) A washer and dryer in the tack room.

26) A refrigerator in the tack room for storing medicines (and sodas!).

27) A large hayloft with hay chutes that open directly into each stall, so that you can easily throw flakes of hay into each stall.

28) Hinged covers on the hay chutes so you can close them in the winter.

29) A seamless hayloft floor built with plywood that will keep dust from filtering down to stalls and aisle below.

30) Hay that is delivered and stacked by someone else.

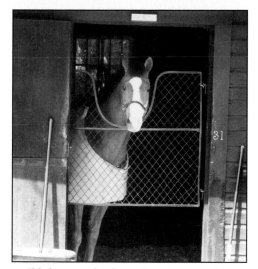

"My horse was lonely—so I spent several nights sleeping with her in the barn."—Contributed by Amanda Slack of Ontario, Canada. —Photo contributed by Lynette Farlow of New York, NY.

"Drummer in my home—a common occurrence!" —Contributed by Chris Harder of Monson, MA.

31) Ventilators on the roof of the barn that help move hot, stuffy air upward and outward.

32) Bedding storage that is easily accessible when you're bedding stalls.

33) Bedding that is always delivered by someone else.

34) Gutters on the barn and good drainage to prevent large pools of standing water and mud around the barn.

35) Level outside paddocks with excellent drainage to keep them fairly dry in all kinds of weather.

36) Acres of turnout fields lush with grass.

37) Safe fencing around the acres of turnout fields and paddocks.

38) Painted metal gates kept in good condition. Rusty, broken down gates can be dangerous.

39) A local farmer just dying to use <u>your</u> manure and willing to haul it away, FREE.

Super Suggestions:

♥ **Keep the phone lines open.** Install a phone in the barn for emergency calls to the vet, so you don't have to leave your babies in a time of crisis. —*Contributed by Shelly Drumheller of Dias Creek, NJ.*

♥ **Keep your ears open.** Set up an intercom system linked directly to the house so you can listen for any unusual noises. —*Contributed by Shelly Drumheller of Dias Creek, NJ.*

♥ **Pipe in their favorite music.** Leave the radio playing softly in the barn to keep them company. —*Contributed by Joyce Aurich of Draper, UT.*

♥ **Add all-around ambience.** Or for better sound, install a stereo system with speakers, inside and out! Check garage sales for a cheap, used stereo. —*Contributed by Laurette Berube of Douglas, MA.*

*"Ahh—keep it coming!" Laramie has her own personal fan to keep cool.
—Photo contributed by Jody Phillips of Hollis, NH.*

*The Clint Goodrich Racing Stable keeps 'em cool at Churchill Downs. Notice the fan in the upper corner
of each stall door. —Photo contributed by Caren Goodrich of Louisville, KY.*

Utopian Stall & Stable

Extra Nuances for the Well-Appointed Stall

Personal Fans

On hot summer days, set up a fan for your stalled horse. If your stall has vertical bars that separate your horse from the aisle, place a large fan flat against the bars and secure it with baling twine. Make sure any excess baling twine and the electrical cord has been taped out of reach of any inquisitive horse lips.

If the ceiling of your barn is very high, fasten a fan to beams and direct the breeze into the stall. The fan must be secured high enough so that even a rearing horse can't reach it.

WHOA:
Always make sure that a fan and its electrical cord are <u>completely</u> out of reach and securely fastened. Check the fan wiring for any frayed cords! Also, don't overload the electrical outlet! Tragic barn fires have been caused by overloading old or poorly-wired systems.

Window Boxes

Hang a a removable window box with brackets over your horse's stall wall or window, and buy several plastic planting trays to fit inside. Use a little Velcro to help the tray stay in place.

Make **Grass Treat Trays**: Fill 2 or 3 plastic lining trays with top soil. Press whole oat or grass seeds firmly into the dirt and let them grow. When the shoots are about 3 - 6 inches tall, drop the plastic planting tray into the window box and let your horse enjoy. Consider staggering the growth days of the sprigs so your horse will have a tasty treat once a week. You can also grow the grass inside your house in the winter for a special, fresh grass treat.

Mary Ellen's Corner
Mary Ellen's window box is outside her stall window. In the summer, she hangs her head out and always finds something special in there for her. In the winter, I move it inside the barn.

Mary Ellen doesn't chew her box. If your horse tends to chew things, you might need to remove the box when you are not in the barn.

Super Suggestions:

- ♥ **Install permanent fans.** For complete luxury, ceiling fans help circulate hot air out. *—Contributed by Lynn Borden of Middletown, NY. Make sure they are installed high enough that even a rearing horse can't touch.*

- ♥ **Serve up Derby Day treats.** In the window box, grow Kentucky Bluegrass and present it to your horse as a special Kentucky Derby Day treat.

- ♥ **Get creative.** Paint or stain the window box. Or purchase several window boxes and paint them for different occasions—Birthday, Christmas or New Year's. Make sure the paint is non-toxic!

- ♥ **Grow aloe for what ails you.** Keep a potted aloe vera plant in the barn. Super for sunburns and other minor ailments that affect both horses and people! *—Contributed by Meghan Pomeroy and Elizabeth Sutton of Ontario, Canada.*

You know your horse is pampered when the barn is cleaner than your home! —Contributed by Andrea Schwarting of Lowville, NY. —Photo contributed by Lynette Farlow of New York, NY.

—Photo contributed by Kendra Bond of Buzzards Bay, MA.

Hunterdon Farms—completely immaculate. George Morris says his pet peeve is anything dirty! —Photo contributed by Lynette Farlow of New York, NY.

Making & Mucking the Perfect Stall

The Imperial Deluxe Suite

Materials:
> Shavings or sawdust
> Straw

Cover the stall floor evenly with 4 - 5 inches of shavings or sawdust. Directly on top, spread a layer of straw evenly about 4 - 6 inches deep. Bank more straw up all sides of the stall to about 1 - 2 feet. Smooth out any uneven bumps in the straw for a finished look.

WHOA:
Straw should have a beautiful gold color and sawdust should smell good, like wood. Neither should smell old or mildewy and both should be as dust-free as possible.

Careful, if you order sawdust directly from a mill—it should be dry. If it is slightly moist and stacked, it can heat up and even spontaneously combust! Also, specify that you do not want any Black Walnut shavings or sawdust. Horses are incredibly sensitive to this type and can easily founder just ingesting only a small amount!

The Presidental Suite

Materials:
> Shavings or sawdust
> Straw

Cover the stall floor evenly with 6 - 10 inches of shavings or sawdust. Then, bank a bale of straw up all sides of the stall to about 1 - 2 feet. The floor of the stall remains shavings or sawdust and the walls, only, are banked with straw.

Mary Ellen's Corner
In the winter, Mary Ellen is bedded in a Presidential Suite and sometimes I substitute hay to make the banks. In the summer, she is bedded in a Simple Suite.

To save money, we order sawdust from a mill. A load that lasts us a year costs about $260 - $300, while the shavings that come in a bag would cost us about $800 or more a year. Before you buy from a mill, however, read the important warning on the left.

Super Suggestions:

❤ **Make it snuggly warm.** In the winter, bank the stall higher with bedding for additional warmth and to cut down on drafts. In the summer, clear away banks to make it cooler.

❤ **Bank up for extra safety.** Banks also help prevent a horse from getting cast in his stall. A horse is cast when he rolls in his stall, gets caught up against a wall, and can't roll back over.

"Her stall is something I fret over ... If I wouldn't want to sleep there, I don't expect her to either."—Contributed by Kathy Weymouth of South China, ME. —Photo contributed by Valarie and Robert Woortman of Lafayette, NJ. Zippos Sonny looks so cozy!

101

Super Suggestions:

💙 **Clear the deck for a hungry horse!** Keep the area under the feed bucket clear of bedding. When the horse drops bits of feed on the floor, he will not pick up bedding trying to eat every kernel off the floor. Feed his hay in this area as well.

💙 **Clear extra space for the extra sloppy eater.** For the less-than-fastidious eater, you may want to keep the entire front of the stall clear under both the water and feed buckets. Spilled water, especially from horses who dunk their hay, just soaks and wastes bedding anyway.

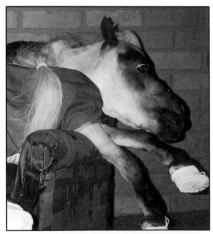

Penelope living the easy life! —Photo contributed by Sandy Larkin of Webster, NY.

The Perfect Stall

"I go through 100 cubic feet of shavings per week!"—Contributed by Linda Singleterry of Paramount, CA.
—Photos contributed by Jo Milliron of Reynoldsburg, OH (left) and Lynette Farlow of New York, NY (right).

Country Suite

Materials:
    Straw

Cover the stall floor evenly with 1 - 2 feet of straw. Smooth out uneven bumps with a rake and bank more straw up sides, about 1 - 2 feet.

Simple Suite

Materials:
    Shavings or sawdust

Cover the stall floor evenly with shavings or sawdust 6 - 10 inches deep and bank more shavings up all sides of the stall, about 1 - 2 feet.

"Chadwick stays outside in a pipe stall with a rubber mat under the shelter. Special flooring is added to build up his paddock area, keeping it drier during the rainy season in California. I even go so far as to channel the dirt and water while it's pouring rain to keep him dry!" —Contributed by Jackie Hahn-Winans of Northridge, CA.

Totally Decadent Skinny Horse Hay Suite

Materials:
> Good quality grass hay

Start with a good, quality grass hay (never economize with moldy or dusty hay). Cover the floor of the stall evenly with about 1 - 2 feet of hay. Smooth out any uneven bumps with a rake.

In some areas, grass hay is an inexpensive alternative to straw. Since most grass hay has less nutritional value than a good quality mix, however, always continue to serve your horse his regular feedings of quality hay. This bedding choice is not recommended if your horse is overweight (he'll eat too much!), on a regimented diet, or has hay allergies.

WHOA:
Again, don't economize by buying moldy or old hay for your horse to sleep on. He will invariably eat some of it. Moldy hay will have a strong musty odor and may have patches of black or white mold. It can cause colic or founder if eaten.

Under-the-Stars No-Frills Suite

Materials:
> Shavings or sawdust

If your stall leads directly out to a paddock, consider just laying rubber matts down in the stall and making a bed outside. Pile shavings or straw about six inches deep directly on the dirt in the paddock.

As the bedding pile becomes dirty, harrow it into the arena or rake it clear. Replace with fresh bedding. Feed your horse inside the stall and just sweep the rubber matts clear each day of dust and dropped grain.

This is a super way to bed your horse luxuriously without the heavy daily work. It works best when you live in a dry climate, such as Arizona. In a wetter climate, of course, you might have problems keeping the outside bedding dry.

—Contributed by Bonnie Ebsen-Jackson, editor of Western Horse magazine, Prescott, AZ. Her horses, Goodman and Nikki, almost always choose to sleep outside under the stars. . . . It's so romantic!

The Perfect Stall

Strip, Bank 'n Muck Method (Major Mucking)

Tools:

    Manure fork
        (tynes close together)
    Hay fork (tynes far apart)
    Shovel
    Broom
    Rake
    Wheelbarrow
    Deodorizer (baking soda, lime
        or stall deodorizer)

First, pick out all visible piles of manure and wet spots. Then, toss the rest of the bedding onto banks against the stall walls. (If your stall already is banked, just toss on top.) Heavier manure balls will drop out of the bedding and roll down the slope of the bank. You can easily shovel them up and toss out. Shovel up wet spots as you find them.

Resift through the bank frequently, tossing it up again, making sure all manure balls have been removed. When the entire stall has been banked, sweep the floor completely clean. Sprinkle on a little deodorizer and let air.

If you are using two types of bedding (straw and shavings as suggested in some of the suites), toss them into separate banks. This will help you clean more thoroughly and creates a neater appearance when you put the stall back together

After the stall has aired sufficiently, fork all the bedding down from the banks and rake smooth. Pick out any missed manure balls and add more bedding if necessary. Rake the oldest bedding into the spot where the horse normally urinates. That way, you can keep his bed as fresh and new as possible.

For a finishing touch, rake the surface of a shavings or sawdust stall flat. Alternately fluff and pat the surface of a straw or hay stall, to give it a flat, neat appearance. If your stall is banked, neaten the banks by running a rake along the topline to give it a straight edge. A bank with a ragged edge will look messy and unkempt.

Quickie Fluff & Muck Method

Pick out all manure and shovel up wet spots that you can easily see. Then, with a pitch fork, turn over and fluff up small sections of bedding. Sift out any manure balls and sweep up wet spots as you find them. Then, evenly rake bedding surface smooth.

For a particularly messy area, toss that particular section onto a bedding bank, letting the manure balls fall out. Scoop them up and toss out. To save bedding around the wet spot, rake as much dry bedding away before shoveling it up.

Stall Freshening

To deodorize, sprinkle baking soda or a dab of Pine Sol onto well-swept wet spots and let air for one hour. For more thorough freshening, sprinkle on a layer of powdered lime and let air for several hours.

Helpful Hint:
If your stalls are not particularly wet, use baking soda or Pine Sol to sprinkle on the stall floor. When lime dries and mixes in with bedding, it can become very dusty.

Once-a-Year Sprucing

Remove feed and water buckets from the stall to keep them free from contaminants. Strip stall of all bedding and discard. Mix a dab of Lysol or Pine Sol disinfectant in a bucket of warm water and scour walls and floor with a long handled scrub brush (or stiff-bristled broom).

Liberally soak area around feed bucket where dribbled grain is caked on. When wet, it's easily loosened with a paint scraper. Scrape the grain off and sweep up thoroughly. Let stall air for several hours with all windows and doors open.

While stall is drying, wash windows and clear away cobwebs or any accumulated dust. Repair any loose boards and nails. When the stall is completely dry, repair any wooden flooring that may be rotted. When all is complete, refill with fresh bedding.

Mary Ellen's Corner
I do my once-a-year sprucing in the fall. That way it is nice and fresh for Mary Ellen since she'll be spending more time in the barn in the winter.

Dust-Free (As Can Be) Aisles

Spray a mist of water beforehand over entire aisle and sweep up dust and debris. Add a little Pine Sol to the water to really freshen.

Immaculate Aisles

You should deep clean cement aisles once a month when the weather is warm to keep fine dust particles under control. First, sweep the floor thoroughly. Then, after dribbling undiluted Pine Sol up and down the aisle, blast away with the hose and spray nozzle on full force towards a drain or out the barn door. Sweep out any puddles, and open all doors and windows to help the floor dry quickly.

On a hot summer day, this can cool the barn by several degrees, especially if a breeze is blowing. If you're experiencing drought conditions or water shortage problems, however, don't use this cleaning technique.

Super Suggestions:

❤ **Be sure to muck as needed.** For a horse who is stalled all day, a Major Mucking every day will keep his bed dry and free of ammonia smells. For horses who get daily turnout, a Quickie Fluff & Muck will do on most days, with a Major Mucking necessary just once or twice a week.

❤ **Make mucking more manageable.** Pick up manure in the stall throughout the day (if you're already in the barn, anyway) and, lastly, in the evening. It will make the cleaning job easier the next day.

❤ **Catch the corners.** Don't neglect the corners of the stall. Fluff them up and clear them out at least every other day. Old bedding left in the corners gets very dusty!

❤ **Keep aisle invaders out.** Never sweep anything from the aisle into a horse's stall. Throw debris in the manure pile or in the garbage.

❤ **Roll in the big guns.** Use a Shop-Vac with a long hose extension to suck up all cobwebs and dust accumulated on ledges.

"Let your horse be a horse—turn him out, let him roll, play, and get dirty."
—Contributed by Jackie Hahn-Winans of Northridge, CA. —Photo contributed by Appaloosa Horse Club of Moscow, ID.

Ultimate

TURNOUT &
INDULGENCES

*Ronald. —Photo contributed by
Meagan Galinger of Valrico, FL.*

*Pine Ridge Indian Reservation.—Photo
contributed by Bernie Hunhoff, publisher of
South Dakota magazine, Yankton, SD.*

*—Photo contributed by Suzanne Drnec of
Hobby Horse Clothing Company, Chino, CA.*

*"I never laugh as much as I do when he's turned out and plays
with his friends. It is so cute to watch happy horses rough-housing with each other."
—Contributed by Jackie Hahn-Winans of Northridge, CA.
—Photo contributed by Kendra Bond of Buzzards Bay, MA.*

Pasture in Paradise

Nothing pampers a horse more than allowing him to be a horse and giving him his freedom to roam. Whether it's in a small dirt paddock or a lush green field, turnout releases tension, reduces nervous habits, and aids in physical and mental health.

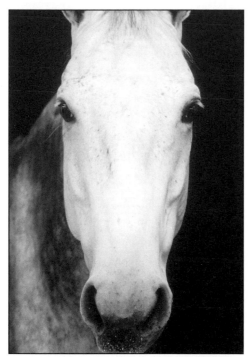

Turn out without a halter. If you must put one on, use a leather halter for extra safety. It will break more easily if it gets caught on anything which reduces the risk of injury to your horse. —Contributed by Anne Bonneville of Gardner, MA.—Photo contributed by Ed Bond.

A wish list for safe and enjoyable turnout

1) Fencing in good condition so horses can't get loose.

2) Fences at least four feet high, and not more than 10 inches from the ground (to prevent foals and small ponies from rolling under).

3) Fresh water supplied in a water tank or clean garbage can, even if there's a pond or stream in the pasture.

4) A salt block provided outside, too.

5) Shade from a run-in shed or trees so horse can seek shelter from sun and heat.

6) Paddocks with good drainage so horses never stand ankle deep in mud and muck.

Mary Ellen's Corner
Everytime our horses are returned to the barn, there is something in their feed buckets—a small amount of feed or just a carrot. When they get loose (and they do get loose) they go directly to the barn looking for that little something to eat!

Super Suggestions:

❤ **Bring along a friend.** Always try to turn your horse out with a buddy. Being herd animals, they might become agitated when turned out alone. If your only horse seems agitated when turned out, a goat can keep him company (or maybe it's time for a second horse!).

❤ **Prevent barnyard rumbles.** When turning out more than one horse, always put out more flakes of hay than there are horses. This way there is always a place for them to eat and no squabbling will erupt.

❤ **Keep your horse bug-free.** See page 119 for economical homemade fly sprays that will help your horse enjoy turnout to the fullest.

—Photo contributed by Mary Jane Ciraco
of Morning Mist Farm, Deland, FL.

"His long life is most assuredly attributed to the fact
that he is never locked in his stall. Rather, he is able
to move from inside to out as he pleases and he
continues to live this lifestyle."—Contributed by
Gretchen Duce of Long Island, NY. She has owned
Albert, a 41 year old Clydesdale/Morgan
cross, for 36 years.

Retired Standardbreds: Natural Image and Nadala. —Photo contributed by Jennifer Volker
of The Standardbred Retirement Foundation, Blairstown, NJ.

Keeping Turnout Trouble-Free

1) Pick up manure in small paddocks to help reduce flies.

2) Harrow larger pastures with a chain attachment to scatter manure piles that attract flies and worms.

3) Mow pastures to keep the weeds trimmed and prevent them from reseeding.

4) Rotate your horses periodically from one field to the next. Rotating helps the lush grass return and prevents worm infestations.

5) Fill woodchuck and rabbit holes to keep horses from slipping in them.

6) Periodically cut out thistles and burrs, before they get caught in your horse's tail.

7) Pick up fallen fruit surrounding fruit trees within reach of your horse. Overindulging in large amounts of fruit can cause horses to colic or founder.

Mary Ellen's Corner
When our paddock gate is opened, it creates a chute from the barn directly to the paddock. We then open the horses' stall doors and they walk out to the paddock themselves. A real-time saver! **Caution:** When letting more than one horse out, let the dominant horse out _last_. This gives the others a chance to get out of the barn and out of the way!

Luxurious Turnout

Indulgent Lush Grass Turnout

Turn out or handwalk your horse in a field with knee-high green grass for 10 - 15 minutes, or longer if your horse is already accustomed to eating green grass.

Suggestion: Allow one small paddock to grow long and lush. Reseed, fertilize (see note below) and water, if necessary. Consider reseeding it with Kentucky Bluegrass. Save this paddock for this special pampering session.

WHOA:
Introduce horses to green grass gradually. Horses can get seriously sick if fed rich green grass when unaccustomed to it.

And, if you fertilize, keep horses out of the paddock until the fertilizer has been absorbed. I usually wait about a month—sometimes more if it hasn't rained. Your local Agricultural Extension can tell you what's best for your area.

Summer Time Rain Dance Turnout

During a gentle summer rain (80 degrees or warmer is suggested) let your horse out to graze. He should be left out only as long as he enjoys it. Afterwards, bring him in and rub him down vigorously with a towel.

—Contributed by Liz Hoskinson of New York, NY.

Snow Angel Pampering Session

Let your horse roll and play in a level field or paddock of untouched snow. They make horsey snow angels when they roll!

—Contributed by Dianne Izbicki of the Horse Care Outlet, Reading, PA.

Mary Ellen's Corner
Mary Ellen loves to be turned out and will jump around her stall if left in too long. If your horse is accustomed to being stabled, however, he may become edgy and nervous when turned out too long. Watch your horse carefully and bring him in if he's uncomfortable.

Super Suggestions:

♥ **Supply extra hay for safety.** Well-fed horses usually will not eat poisonous plants. If your pasture is sparse, however, you might want to feed extra hay to ensure that your horse does not start nibbling at inedible plants in hunger.

♥ **Put on your snow shoes.** If you can't turn your horse out in the snow, just lead your horse out on a leadline so he can put his nose in it! —*Contributed by Faith Livermore of Land O' Lakes, FL.*

Covered in snow. —Photo contributed by Stephanie Peddicord of Bits & Bridles Saddlery, Ellicott City, MD.

Super Suggestion:

♥ **Make sure he's a happy camper.**
Some horses may become nervous if they are not used to being turned out. Keep an eye on your horse and bring him in if he shows any discomfort. Turn him out with a buddy whenever possible.

Since show horses can spend hours in their stalls, the horses at Ri-Arm Farm are hand-walked up to 2 - 3 hours per day at one hour intervals. —Contributed by Steve Weiss, barn manager of Mark Leone's Ri-Arm Farm, Oakland, NJ. —Photo contributed by Lynette Farlow of New York, NY.

112

Luxurious Turnout

Evening Turnout

When the days are too hot and buggy for turnout, try night time turnout. This way you can leave your horse in the barn during the day away from bugs and heat, and out at night when it's bug-free.

Your horse can stay out from late afternoon until the next morning. Serve extra hay in sparse paddocks, as hungry horses will find a way out of the paddock or pasture in search of food.

Suggestion: If you're worried about leaving your horse out overnight without supervision, just turn him out until 11:00 PM or so. He'll appreciate the cool, less-buggy summer breezes.

—*Contributed by Joanne Dzenkowski, a groom with Anne Kursinski, Flemington, NJ.*

WHOA:
For evening turnout, be especially sure your fields are in good condition. Check for holes frequently and, above all, check to make sure your fencing is in excellent condition.

Delta's delight: Piles of hay at her feet.

Mountain O' Hay Turnout

On a cold fall or winter day, open several more bales of hay than you usually do. Spread the hay around in heaping piles. Let the horses luxuriate in knee or thigh-high mountains of hay. It's great on Christmas morning!

WHOA:
Thick, wooly horses who have not been blanketed can stay out as long as they wish in cold weather. Horses who have been clipped will need protection with blankets.

Total Indulgence

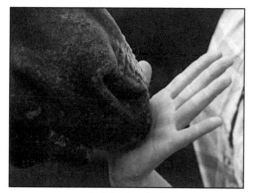

Satisfaction check.

Mud Bath Treatment

In very warm weather, spray a section of a dry paddock with water. Let the sun warm it up. Turn your horse out and let him roll luxuriously. Add some hay so he can eat between rolls. Bring him in and curry him vigorously after he dries. The mud will bring out a glossy shine!

Option: On a particularly muddy day after a rain, simply turn him out for a roll in the mud.

—*Contributed by Teri Shaw of Ashland, OH.*

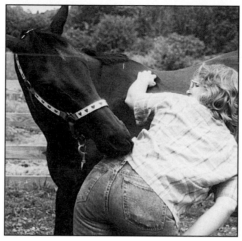

Careful of little nips!

Mutual Grooming

Attach a lead shank to your horse's halter and allow him to continue grazing. Stand at his shoulder and face his rear end. Scratch his back, shoulder, withers and belly with a curry comb or just with your fingertips.

Satisfaction Check: To make sure he is enjoying the mutual grooming session, reach around to his nose and let him "groom" your hand by twitching his lips. He may even lean around and scratch your back with his nose for the full mutual grooming experience (careful of little nips).

Super Suggestion:

❤ **Shake, wriggle, and roll.** Many of the "spa" treatments in this chapter suggest allowing your horse to roll. Rolling helps horses groom themselves, aids in stimulating skin, massages muscles, and assists in spring shedding. It also feels good!

"Our mutual greeting—I pop a piece of Dentyne in my mouth, he puts his nose up to mine, and I gently blow Dentyne breath in his nose. He loves it. Go figure!" —Contributed by Mary Welch of Lawrenceville, GA.

—Photo contributed by Suzanne Drnec of Hobby Horse Clothing Company, Chino, CA.

Total Indulgence

Ultimate Spa Massage

To begin, cross-tie your horse away from any distractions and noises. Peace and quiet are essential.

Start with his face. Holding your index, middle and ring fingers firmly together, rub in small circles over his entire face. Rub firmly over the meaty areas and more gently over eyelids and around the muzzle.

Then, massage down his neck with the heel of your palm. Press your palm into the muscle and rotate it. Follow through on his shoulder and work your way back to his hindquarters. For extra stiff muscles, gently pat the muscle masses flatly with your fingers while continuing the rotating palm motion. Once you have finished one side, repeat it on the other side.

—Photo contributed by Samantha Hartford of Chapel Hill, NC. She took an Equine Sports Massage course so she could massage Lestat with expertise.

After you have finished the body, massage his neck and spine. With the tips of your fingers, rub the muscles on each side of the crest of his mane in small circles, starting in between the ears. Continue over his withers and the entire length of his spine, including the large muscle masses over his back and where the tail begins. Do both sides of the spine equally.

Then, on to the legs. Remember, safety first! Never kneel or sit. Always squat or bend over to work.

Start with the upper part of the leg and work in either a circular or an up-and-down motion with a stiff, flat hand pressed against the leg. Become more gentle as you work on his knee and lower leg. Use your fingertips to gently massage tendons, ankles, and around topline of the hoof at the coronet band and heel. Report any heat or sensitivity that you feel to your trainer or vet.

For a little extra pampering, apply a small amount of liniment to your palm and massage into the large muscle masses as well as the entire leg. Use only a small amount of liniment, as some sensitive horses can blister when too much liniment is rubbed in too vigorously.

Remember: Use consistent and soft movements. Jerky or sudden hand movements will only disturb or frighten him. Press firmly on the fleshier parts of the horse and lighter on more sensitive or ticklish areas. Ticklish areas may cause a horse to jump or even kick. Be alert and always stand in a safe position well out of kicking range! And, remember, this is a relaxing massage. You are rubbing too hard if your horse shows any sign of discomfort.

Put your head on my shoulder ... —Photo contributed by JoAnn Putnam of Vienna, VA.

Quickie Reassuring Hug

Train your horse slowly to lower his head and press his face flat against your chest. Stroke his face and neck gently. Talk to him as you reassure.

Mary Ellen's Corner
Mary Ellen was very head shy when I first got her. For several months, I coaxed her to put her head down. This technique, as well as the face grooming on page 21 and facial massage on page 23, have made her more accepting of things around her head.

Cool Towel Spa Curry for Hot Days

Moisten a towel with cool water and wring it out completely. Wrap the towel around your hand like a glove. Curry the entire horse, rubbing his coat in small circles and removing dirt as well. Rinse and wring out towel frequently. Apply a little fly spray to the towel as well—for a little de-bugging!

Warm Towel Spa Rubdown

Materials:

    Styrofoam cooler
    Dryer
    2 - 3 plush towels

Put dry towels in the dryer and let them spin for 10 - 20 minutes. Take them out and immediately cover in a styrofoam cooler to hold in the warmth. Rub your horse down with the warm towels. As soon as one towel cools off, use another. Great if he accidentally gets caught in a cool rain!

Super Suggestions:

- **Lift those confinement blues.** Pay extra attention to a confined or quarantined horse. Visit him several times during the day and spend extra time stroking him, talking to him, and grooming. If he can be handwalked, encourage him to roll in a soft spot while still on the lead linc. —*Contributed by Leslie Webb of Bakersfield, CA. Leslie competes internationally, and her horses are frequently quarantined due to the travel.*

- **Get the low-down on a rub-down.** For the ultimate massage, hire a certified equine massage therapist for your horse. Your stable or tack store should be able to help you find one. —*Contributed by Moira Harris, editor of Horse Illustrated of Mission Viejo, CA.*

"Happiness is grazing in the lush green grass outside his dirt paddock!"—Contributed by Mary Welch of Lawrenceville, GA.

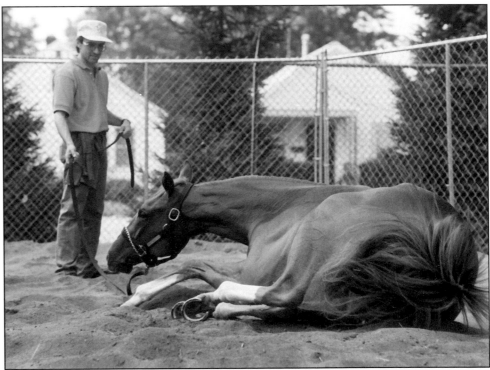

Trail Dust, a 2-year-old Thoroughbred, in his sand box with trainer Clint Goodrich. Rolling is like a refreshing back scratch and can be a remedy for training aches and pains. —Photo contributed by Caren Goodrich of Lousiville, KY.

Total Indulgence

Full Body Sand Box Shake

Let your horse roll after a workout in a sandy paddock. If you don't have one, have a load of sand delivered to a spot outside the barn and rake it smooth into a rolling pit for your horse. Make sure it's deep—10 inches or so, especially if it's covering cement. After a workout, take your horse out for a roll in the sand.

To teach a horse to roll on the end of a lead shank, just let him circle around you on the end of the leadline in the sand pit. It's natural for a horse to lay down and roll, but some horses take a little time before they realize that they can do it right then and there.

After the horse gets up, he usually does a full body shake to knock off the sand clinging to him. A full body shake not only gets excess sand off, it can also help realign the spine.

Rolling in a sandy paddock after a workout will absorb sweat and hasten drying. —Contributed by Suzanne Marchi of Wild Oak Farm, Chicago Park, CA. —Photo contributed by Charlene Strickland of Bosque Farms, NM.

If he does not shake, teach him. Pick up 3 - 4 hairs from the base of his mane near the withers, and tug gently to create a tickle. The horse will usually respond to the tickle and shake. If the horse does not respond within a minute or so, you can take an open safety pin and gently tickle the top of his withers with the point of the pin. This tickling nearly always gets a quick response.

—Contributed by Caren Goodrich of Louisville, KY. Horses in training at the racetrack don't have the freedom to enjoy the simple pleasures of pasture turnout, so Caren and Clint created a "playpen" for their racehorses as a way to help them unwind after a morning workout.

Mathilda can roll all the way over. —Photos contributed by Katherine Walcott of Wilsonville, AL.

Turned out yearlings. —Photo contributed by Judy Decker of Johnson, NY.

As Bug-Free As Can Be!

Before any turnout in buggy weather, protect your horse with fly spray. Pay particular attention to his legs and belly. Do not spray directly on your horse's face, however. Instead, spray on a cloth and wipe his face and around his eyes. Or rub a <u>thin</u> layer of Clear Swat around each eye (careful not to get any in the eyes).

Apply a small amount of petroleum jelly, Clear Swat, mineral oil, or even straight Avon Skin So Soft just inside their ear flaps to prevent highly irritating gnats from biting. If you use mineral oil or Avon Skin So Soft, apply it with a cloth or cotton ball to prevent it from running down into the ear canal. Always wipe upward and outward when applying anything inside the ear.

Mary Ellen's Corner
Our farrier reports that some hoof cracks are caused by incessant stamping at flies in very dry conditions. With that in mind, I spray Mary Ellen's legs with an oilier spray and use a lighter spray on her body. The oily spray seems to cling to her legs better and last longer. I don't use the oily spray on her body, however, because it makes her hot and sweaty.

For added protection, apply Clear Swat directly to the skin around his sheath or her udders, and to the crease down the middle of their bellies (their midline) to their belly buttons.

Apple Cider Bug-Be-Gone

Try an apple cider vinegar dip. Mix 1 - 2 cups apple cider vinegar with a bucket of warm water, then sponge the entire horse and let dry. The smell of the vinegar keeps the flies away.

Or, feed 1/2 cup apple cider vinegar daily to reduce the number of flies attracted to your horse. Flies will not be attracted to the manure of vinegar fed horses.

—*Contributed by Phyllis Hubbard of Corydon, IN. Be sure to feed real apple cider vinegar, and not an imitation.*

Beau. —Photo contributed by Karen Stotka of North Providence, RI.

119

Super Suggestions:

❤ **Keep flies from their eyes.** Fly masks can be helpful. If your horse is turned out at night, though, be sure to remove it.

❤ **Chase away flies with an after-bath splash.** Mix one part Jean Naté with 4 - 5 parts water in a clean spray bottle and splash lightly to help keep the flies away. Be careful not to get any in their eyes.
—*Contributed by Diana Christie of San Martin, CA.*

Fringed fly bonnets help keep flies away from their eyes. Isn't it becoming on Delta! —Photo contributed by Judy Decker of Johnson, NY.

Be Bug-Free!

Jolene's Homemade Fly Repellent

Ingredients:
> 2 cups white vinegar
> 1 cup Avon Skin So Soft Bath Oil (original scent)
> 1 cup water
> 1 tablespoon eucalyptus oil

Mix ingredients together in a spray bottle. Apply to your horse before turning out. Reapply as needed, as it will wear off as the horse sweats or rolls.

—*Contributed by Jolene Venables of Canoga Park, CA. Jolene's Horse Rescue operation is well-known for saving and finding new homes for abused horses.*

Eucalyptus Fly Bath

Mix the ingredients of Jolene's Homemade Fly Repellent in a bucket of warm water and rinse horse off completely to repel flies.

Author's Note:
For a detangler and fly repellent for tails, see *page 29!*

Garlic Bug Chasers

To help thwart bugs, crush one garlic clove and mix in with his daily feed.
—*Contributed by Joan Thompson of Brownsville, OR.*

Or add one teaspoon powdered garlic at each feeding.
—*Contributed by Lesley Ward, editor of Young Rider magazine, Mission Viejo, CA.*

Author's Note:
We're not sure whether it's the garlic scented sweat or possibly their breath that chases the flies away, but many people have written in to praise the benefits of garlic.

Call in the Fly Busters!

Enlist the help of nature's round-the-clock fly patrol—bats and chickens. Installing bat houses in your barn to help attract these nocturnal bug-eaters. During the day, free-roaming chickens will also help keep the fly population down.

—*Contributed by Diana Christie of San Martin, CA. With her crackerjack team of bats and chickens on the job, she has reduced her fly spray use by 75%.*

Author's Note:
Barn Swallows also eat mosquitos, so don't tear down their mud nests from the beams inside your barn.

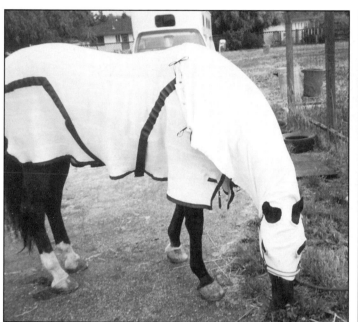 

Make your own fly bonnet! On the left is Rags in his "snood," and on the right is Rascal in his bug-rebuffing cover-up.
—Photos contributed by Diana Christie of San Martin, CA (left) and Marcy Gamester of Westford, MA (right).

❤ **Let your horse run over traffic cones, too.** Traffic cones make great toys! Your horse will love chewing them, shaking them, and stomping all over them. The big, soft rubber ones are best. (Don't use the smaller ones made of hard plastic.) —*Contributed by Gaye Huettner of Cal Gaye Ranch, Paso Robles, CA.*

—Photo contributed by Gaye Huettner of Cal Gaye Ranch, Paso Robles, CA.

Toys: A Must for the Pampered Horse

Playing with toys helps horses overcome boredom and encourages exercise. There are many terrific horse toys available on the market; and here are some homemade alternatives your horse might also enjoy.

—Photo contributed by Ileen Green of North Miami, Fl. She has created a thriving business selling the Horsey Hang-Up, based on a toy she originally made for her own horse.

Bean Bag Boredom-Buster

Materials:
  1 old pillowcase
  1 - 2 bags dry red chili beans
  Apple scented spray

Pour the beans into the empty pillowcase. Sew up the open end of the pillow and spray with an apple or molasses scented spray, such as EZ Bit. Toss it on the floor of the stall for the horse to play with, or tie it to the ceiling. To do so, knot baling twine around a corner of the pillow (do not cut a hole in the pillow case, as your horse will just rip it down after one tug). Loop the twine around a rafter or ceiling beam. Do not tie to a nail that can pull out and become lost in the stall.

—*Contributed by Meagan Galinger of Valrico, FL.*

Turnip Turn-Ons

Material:

    3 turnips
    Baling twine

Choose big turnips that are too large to fit in your horse's mouth in one piece. Core each one so there is a hole that goes all the way through. Tic turnips together by running baling twine through the holes and tying ends of baling twine in a knot. Tie it high enough in the stall so your horse can't get a foot into the toy, but he can reach it to nibble at it. Tie to a rafter or beam. Do not tie it to a nail that can be pulled out and lost in the stall. *Remove this toy when unsupervised!*

Or simply put a large turnip in his feed bucket for him to push around.

—*Contributed by DeAnn Schott of Costa Mesa, CA.*

WHOA:
Our vet has approved both beans and turnips, but check with yours to make sure that they are okay for your horse.

Know your horse and what can be left with him. We recommend that toys like the Turnip Turn-Ons be removed when no one is in the barn, just to be on the safe side. Besides, horses tire of a toy left with them constantly. When it's brought back again, they'll think it's something new.

Truck mud flaps secured to a fence make terrific scratchers. Here we see Sonoma Cinco, a 4-month-old filly, scratching an itchy spot on one.
—*Photo contributed by Karen McMillen and Gail Reifers of Talawind Ranch, Windsor, CA.*

Morgan Stallion Willo Pond Knight Rebel plays with a Horseball. —*Photo contributed by JoAnn Anderson of Blue Hills Lippitt Morgans, Exeland, WI.*

Super Suggestions:

💙 **Milk the containers for all they're worth.** Hang clean one-gallon plastic milk jugs in the stall or from fence posts. Hang them singularly or in groups of three for something extra to bang around.
—*Contributed by Karen McMillen and Gail Reifers of Talawind Ranch, Windsor, CA.*

💙 **Let 'em toy with timber.** Make a toy out of a truck load of sawdust dumped in a dirt paddock.
—*Contributed by Karen McMillen and Gail Reifers of Talawind Ranch, Windsor, CA. Their horses have a blast rolling and spreading it around.*

Sassy Fass preparing to roll in a sawdust pile. —*Photo contributed by Karen McMillen and Gail Reifers of Talawind Ranch, Windsor, CA.* **123**

Smooth 'n Easy Guy playing with a Horseball. We had
to give him a whole page—he's having so much fun!
—Photos contributed by Eck Quarter Horses
of Manassas, VA.

Toys

Incredibly edible or edibly incredible. —Photo contributed by Jackie Hahn-Winans of Northridge, CA.

Jug of Oats

Clean out a plastic milk jug and pour in one cup of oats. Cut a tiny hole in the bottom of the jug, small enough for one or two oat kernels to fall out. Leave the cap off and tie it to a rafter or ceiling beam with baling twine, and let your horse enjoy. Do not tie it to a nail, as the nail may pull out and become lost in the stall.

—Contributed by Erin Appleyard of Ontario, Canada.

Jackie's Incredible Edible Christmas Wreath

Select seven red and seven green apples and 3 - 4 carrots. Arrange the apples in alternating colors and intersperse the carrots throughout. Pierce each apple and carrot through the center with a straightened coat hanger. Fashion the wire loaded with fruit in a circle and twist the excess wire into a knot at the top. Cut off any extra wire and wrap duct tape around the wire ends so there are no sharp edges. Makes a delightful toy treat and decoration at Christmas!

—Contributed by Jackie Hahn-Winans of Northridge, CA.

Commakaze, an Arab/Mustang filly, playing with a cardboard box. —Photo contributed by Karen McMillen and Gail Reifers of Talawind Ranch, Windsor, CA.

Super Suggestions:

♥ **Raid Bowser's toy chest.** Hang a large rubber dog chew toy in your horse's stall for tension-relieving fun. Why should dogs have all the chewing satisfaction? *—Contributed by Fay Seltzer of Natural High Farm, Orwigsburg, PA. Make sure the toy is large enough that your horse won't accidentally swallow it.*

♥ **Deliver romp'em, stomp'em fun.** Empty cardboard boxes! They can pick them up, throw them around and stomp on them. *—Contributed by Karen McMillen and Gail Reifers of Talawind Ranch, Windsor, CA. Remove any staples first, as box staples are sharp and painful if stepped on or eaten. And, if it is secured with tape, make sure the pieces are not loose.*

Entertain friends and family with hours of videos and pictures of your horse. They're all so photogenic! —Contributed by Jane Roane of Magnolia Paso Fino Farm, Nesbit, MS. —Photo contributed by Judy Decker of Johnson, NY.

Throw a party just for him because he deserves it! —Photo contributed by Jolene Venables of Jolene's Horse Rescue, Canoga Park, CA.

Ultimate

PARTIES & GAMES

"On his birthday, I let him get as dirty as he wants."
Rory (boy) and Herbie (pony), both covered
in mud.—Contributed by Ingrid Finnegan
of Chester, NY.

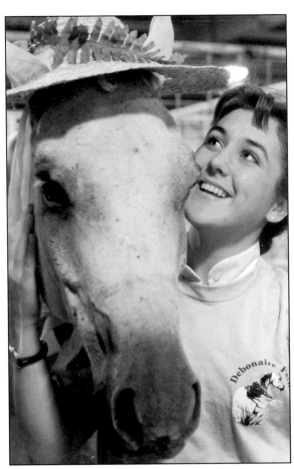

Sarah Bruns and Silver, a 10-year-old Arabian.
—Photo contributed by Kristy Bruns of Prairie Song Designs,
Valley Center, KS.

—Photo contributed by Elaine Smith of Marrero, LA.

—Photo contributed by Laura
Lopresti of The Tack Shelter,
Colts Neck, NJ.

128

Ultimate Parties

Mad Hatter Birthday Party

Invite each guest to buy or make exotic hats for themselves and their horse to wear at the party. After everyone has arrived, judge the duo with the best hats. Also, judge the horse that shows the most manners and patience for wearing and riding with a hat!

Hat Idea: A thrift shop will have a wealth of old-fashioned, inexpensive hats for you and your horse.

Party Idea: Invite your party goers to make hats out of things horses would eat, such as; hay, apples, carrots, etc. Try a craft store for plastic fruit and create a Carmen Miranda look!

Booby Prize: You can also have a booby prize for horses who get huffy over the indignity of it all. Perhaps extra carrots to mollify their feelings.

Patient Delta is a prime prospect for hat-wearing. Decorate with silk flowers and tie to the head with satin ribbon (or baling twine). I've stapled the ribbon to the brim of the hat on each side. For safety, always cover the staples with tape.

WHOA:
Don't force your horse to wear a hat if he doesn't want. Just wear one yourself. And, make sure your horse sees the hat and becomes accustomed to you in it before you ride.

If you make your hat out of edible horse foods, make sure the horses are not allowed to eat them. Party goers may have used glue or pins to hold the hats together.

Remember, don't let your horse overindulge in treats at any party. Feed them only in moderation! And, above all, remove hats from unattended horses.

Super Suggestions:

❤ **Size up the event.** Make sure there is enough room for your party. Have it outside or in an indoor arena if your barn aisle is too narrow.

❤ **Display that old-fashioned hospitality.** If you are inviting people and horses from nearby barns, provide buckets of water, hay, additional turnout or bedded stalls—just in case.

❤ **Keep Nervous Nellies at home.** Never bring a nervous horse to a large party. Introduce him to a smaller party at home first. Or borrow a calm school horse who would probably love the attention.

❤ **Tag potential party-poopers.** Tie a red ribbon to a nervous or excitable horse's tail as a reminder to everyone to keep clear. She might kick.

Mary Ellen always wears a ribbon at parties.

Ultimate Parties

Hat-In-A-Minute Birthday Party

Buy enough party hats for horses and humans. Wear the hats around the barn and outside riding, or just let the hatted horses hang their heads out of their stalls. Makes a terrific picture!

On the hats for the horses, replace the elastic band with two pieces of colorful satin ribbon 18 inches long so they can be tied to the horses' heads. Staple the ribbon from the inside out and cover the staples with a small piece of tape.

Make Your Own Party Hats:

1) Roll a piece of poster board into a cone shape. Leave a one inch wide-hole at the narrow end. Tape the sides together.

2) Cut two pieces of ribbon 18 inches long. Staple them to the opposite sides of the wide end of the cone. This will hold the hat on the horse's head. Again, staple from the inside out and cover staples with a small piece of tape.

For In-A-Minute party hats, store-bought hats are easiest. They are simple to prepare and most horses will wear them with no problem.

3) To make a tassel that will come out of the top of the hat, bundle a handful of hay, add streamers or ribbons. Tape one end tightly together.

4) Insert the taped end of the bundle through the small hole open at the top of the cone. Duct tape it to the inside of the cone.

Here I am struggling to put an overly large hat on Delta. We recommend smaller hats which are much more manageable and more likely to be tolerated. —Photos contributed by Judy Decker of Johnson, NY.

Invitation Idea:

1) Invite your guests to make and decorate birthday hats themselves and wear them to the party! Award a prize for the best one.

WHOA:
Remember, only invite gentle horses who will not mind wearing a hat. Easily spooked horses will spoil the party and could even hurt themselves. And remove hats from unattended horses. Don't forget to accustom your horse to you wearing a hat as well.

Holiday Horse Charity Fundraising Gala

Label several large shipping boxes with the address of a local horse-oriented charity. Or, address each box to a different charity.

Invited guests are encouraged to bring a donation. Donations can be anything from a check to a feed bucket, or even a clean used item. Each guest puts their gift in the box.

As a box is filled, it's sealed at the party and everyone celebrates with a toast: Glasses of sherry for adults, soda for kids and treats for the horses!

Extra Idea: Contact the charity beforehand and find out what they need most, or the type of donations that would be most helpful. Then either include a wish list from the charity in the invitation or register the wish list with your local tack and feed store.

Charities Who Would Love to Participate:

1) Jolene's Horse Rescue
7218 Owensmouth Avenue
Suite 416
Canoga Park, CA 91303
(818) 734-9664

2) Standardbred Retirement Foundation
PO Box 57
Blairstown, NJ 07825
(908) 362-9084

3) Ryerss Farm for Aged Equines
1710 Ridge Rd.
Pottstown, PA 19465
(610) 469-0533

4) Thoroughbred Retirement Foundation
1050 Hwy 35, Suite 351
Shrewsbury, NJ 07702
(908) 957-0182

There are countless charities across the country who greatly appreciate any help they can get. You can find a charity close to your home by contacting The American Horse Council at (202) 296-4031. Their directory lists a wide variety of equine welfare organizations.

Super Suggestions:

- **Throw an instant party.** Have a casual party right in your aisle! Attach a bucket filled with apples and carrots to the barn wall. Tack up an invitation honoring the birthday horse. Invite everyone to take a bite from the goodies in the bucket. *—Contributed by Lynda Hamilton of Santa Rosa, CA.*

- **Dress up for the occasion.** Outfit your horse in a brightly colored halter and lead shank for the festive occasion.

- **Make parties convenient for all.** Always be considerate of traveling and trailering guests. Plan your party during the day when driving and riding is easiest!

Mini, in the car, on the go! —Contributed by Ugell and Lynn Ingles of Sorento, IL.

Super Suggestions:

💛 **Light up your horse!** Purchase battery-powered Christmas lights (available at craft stores). Attach the battery packet to your saddle with baling twine. Run the lights up your horse's mane and secure them with red and green ribbons. Introduce these lights slowly before you attach them to the mane. Only use this decorating idea on an incredibly patient and well-mannered horse.

💛 **Add colorful holiday cheer.** Wrap garland up and around the saddle for an additional holiday effect.
—*Contributed by Mary Jane Ciraco of Morning Mist Farm, Deland, Fl.*

💛 **Achieve local notoriety.** Invite your local newspaper to attend your dress-up or hat parties. Provides great exposure for a boarding stable or pony club.

💛 **Mix some fun with schooling.** Some of these parties can be turned into classes at a horse show or fundraising events.

Ultimate Parties

Christmas Trail Ride & Antler Party

Buy enough antler sets for each horse and rider. (You can find antlers that are specifically made for horses at your tack store.) Mail a set of antlers along with the invitation, or mention in the invitation that antlers will be available for each guest at the party. All party-goers, ride along a pre-planned route spreading Christmas cheer and caroling to neighbors (go ahead: human nickering and neighing allowed!). When you return, serve warm cider to everyone on horseback and toast the holidays.

Make Your Own Antlers:

1) Use flat, uncreased cardboard and cut out the antler shape you wish. (Or use the template at right.)

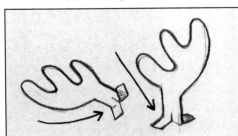

(Step 3) Antler stabilizers: Make cuts into antler bottoms to keep them from flopping over. Bend one piece forward and one back. Wrap a pipe cleaner around it.

2) Duct tape pipe cleaners to the back of the antlers to help hold the shape. Reinforce the back of heavier cardboard with extra pipe cleaners.

3) Tape two additional pipe cleaners extending below the bottom of each antler. Then, cut straight up into the card board to make a "stabilizer." (See diagram bottom left.) Bend one forward and one back. The pipe cleaners and card board stabilizers will twist around the brow band or crown piece of your bridle. Use an extra pipe cleaner to wrap around for more stability and keep the antlers from flopping over. For humans, attach to a sturdy head band or ear muffs over the hard hat.

Extra Idea: If you would prefer not be a reindeer, you can be an angel instead. Use pipe cleaners to make a halo, and twist in gold garland to make it look like it glows!

Mary Ellen's Corner
When attaching anything to your horse's head or mane, always show him the item. Even if it takes several days, gently and patiently accustom him to it. I show Mary Ellen the new item first and then rub her with it. Anytime she gets nervous, I back up a step to let her smell it. If your horse is too spooky, try a reliable school horse so you'll be able to join in on all the fun!

Adapt horsey antlers for people by threading a piece of ribbon through the openings meant for the bridle. Tie it securely to your head as above. Make sure your horse sees you wearing this before you hop on his back! (They are actually quite warm. Great for chilly days!)

Delta modeling her homemade antlers. You can make them bigger or smaller. Delta looks particularly funny in small ones as she has such a big head!

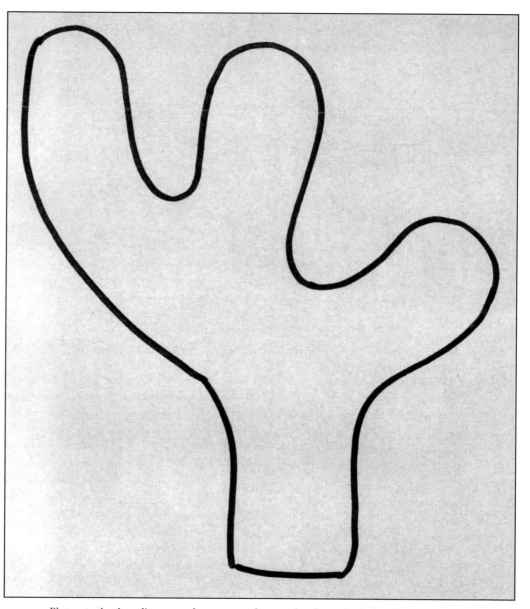

Photo copy the above diagram and cut out to make a template for tracing both right and left antlers. To make them larger, just size up the diagram about 110% - 130% (or as large as you want) on a photocopying machine before tracing the outline onto the cardboard.

"My husband just shakes his head and exclaims, 'You would think they're million-dollar racehorses!' I'd work two jobs if I had to!" —Contributed by Mary Jane Ciraco of Morning Mist Farm, Deland, FL. —Photo contributed by Liz Merrill of Cape Porpoise, ME.

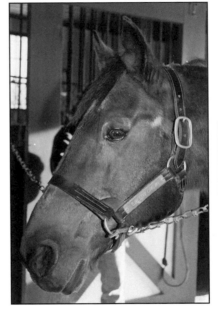

Million-dollar Thoroughbred race horse—invaluable! —Photo contributed by Del Mar Thoroughbred Club racetrack of Del Mar, CA.

Champion Standardbred breeding stallion, Speedy Crown—priceless! —Photo contributed by Judy Decker of Johnson, NY.

John Crump's 10-year-old Percheron, Ann—irreplaceable! —Photo contributed by Melinda Crump of Crump's Leather Shop, Bowling Green, KY.

Ultimate Parties

Halloween & Costume Parties

Invite both horse and rider to come dressed up and award the best costume.

Party Idea: Come dressed up as a matching team. Bride and groom, ballet dancers in tutus, Pony Express team, racehorse and jockey, pair of angels, matching clowns, Blues Brothers, Romeo and Juliet, Santa Claus and Rudolph, Santa and Mrs. Claus, or Robin Hood and Maid Marion. The options are endless!

Party Idea: Or invite everyone to a black tie costume party. Add pearls to the mares and big bow ties to the geldings. Use your imagination with black fabric to create fabulous outfits!

Party Idea: To be really goofy, name your Halloween party a Horse-O-Ween party. Guests (people and horses) are Horse-O-Weenies!
—*Contributed by Darlene Williams of Green Valley Tack, Pine Island, NY.*

Auction Party & Benefit

Set up the barn or "auction room" like an exclusive Sotheby's auction. Create a podium with tack trunks and arrange chairs in rows facing the podium. Use a hammer or rubber mallet as a gavel.

Invite your guests to bring an inexpensive gift, wrapped elaborately using anything uncommon or even bizarre! (Be sure to suggest on the invitation what they should spend on the gift—$10 - 20, $20 - 30, or whatever. This way everyone knows beforehand the approximate value of the mystery items they're bidding on.)

Then, auction off each box to the highest bidder. The money is donated to a horse charity and the winning bid receives the wrapped gift. The "auctioneer" should start

No costume needed! And, boy do they look sharp. Leopard Appaloosa and Dalmations.
—*Photo contributed by Peggy Ann Strupp of Redrock Dalmations, Soda Springs, ID.*

the bidding for each item at a fraction of the estimated value to get the bidding excitement going—and should encourage whoops and yells from the crowd as the bids get higher.

To encourage elaborate wrapping, the person whose gift brings in the most money wins a special prize or a gift certificate from a tack store!

Party Idea: The more people, the better!

Ultimate Parties

Get the spirit and decorate everything! —Photo contributed by Michelle Simpson of Claremore, OK.

A Paul Revere Ride-A-thon

Plan a ride on April 18th or as close to that day as possible to commemorate Paul Revere's famous ride.

Suggest everyone wear red, white and blue (or colonial garb) in honor of the Revolutionary War and Paul Revere. Add matching saddle pads, polo wraps, ribbons in braided manes, etc!

Extra ideas: Ride for fun or organize it as a benefit and work for sponsorship per mile you ride. Or volunteer to participate in a Memorial Day or Fourth of July parades.

Helpful Hint:
Remember, limit the miles ridden to the fitness of your horse. Arrange check points where you can water and rest your horse. If you do ride into town, be sure to check with your local police. They may even help with traffic!

Tack Cleaning Party

Invite friends over to chat and clean their tack. Set up in your kitchen, tack room, or just about anywhere. Provide saddle soap, sponges, buckets, rags, neatsfoot oil, lexol and hot water. Serve snacks and soda. For kids, try a tack cleaning slumber party.

—Contributed by June Laughlin of Bedford, VA. Some cleaning suggestions you can try: to loosen crud on bits and stirrups, drop a denture tablet into a bucket of warm water and let soak. Or polish bits with toothpaste (it tastes better than metal polish). Scrub girth elastic gently with a toothbrush and Ajax cleaner and then rinse clean.

Party Idea: Ask a local tack store to sponsor a tack cleaning party outside their store. They might be able to get manufacturers to visit and provide samples of new products to try. Encourage your tack store to invite everyone on their mailing list. It's a great way to meet horse people and, of course, clean grungy tack!

Helpful Hint:
In fact, invite your local tack shop to participate with any of the parties in this section. It will be great fun for you and terrific publicity for them!

Follow the Map Picnic Party

Map out a fun trail ride that winds through the woods leading to the picnic. Don't tell the guests the exact location of the picnic—make them follow the map instead! Make sure your map and directions are clear enough to ensure that all riders reach the destination safely and within a reasonable time. For extra fun, send out riders in pairs at five-minute intervals, instead of riding out together as a group.

Party Idea: Invite another local stable to meet for the picnic, too. Send them a map prior to the date with a different trail ride. For excitement, allow the two different routes to criss-cross.

WHOA:

Make sure all invited guests are able to ride safely to the party—no dangerous highways, intersections, overpasses, etc! And, if jumps are included, make sure that there is a safe way around just in case someone doesn't want to jump!

Make sure there is plenty of water at the picnic site for thirsty horses.

Bubba was orphaned as a foal and Union Card, a gelding, took over the mothering. —Photo contributed by Sue Harper of Harper Farms, LaGrange, OH.

Foal Shower

Plan a wishing well party. Decorate an empty water bucket in pink and blue crepe paper. Encourage guests to bring inexpensive gifts (for the foal, of course) to drop into the wishing well. Open the gifts in front of the mare at a table and chairs set up in front of the stall.

—Contributed by Melinda Moore of Grants Pass, OR.

Invitation Idea: Purchase the <u>smallest</u> horseshoes available from your blacksmith (or make baby horseshoes out of cardboard). Punch a small hole through the corner of the written invitations, and string the horse shoe to the invitation with pink and blue satin ribbons. Mail in padded envelopes available at your post office.

Kitty and Aiko, a 3-week-old Azteca (Andalusian and Quarter Horse cross). —Photo contributed by Lynn Wolf of Back in the Saddle Catalog Company, Durango, CO.

Quarter Horses, Rose and Cody. —Photo contributed by Melinda Moore of Grants Pass, OR.

Other Parties

Plan a Bake-Off Party and have a bake sale with the treats. For extra profits sell human treats as well!
—Photo contributed by Lisa Miller of Corrales, NM.

Delta taste-testing. Big, juicy Rome apples are the best.

Johnny Appleseed Treat Party

Invite each guest to bring a homemade treat made from apples. Guests are invited to make both human and horse treats.

Invitation Idea: Purchase small baskets (one for each guest) that can fit one or two apples. Write the invitation details on a card, place in basket with the apples, add a red ribbon bow, and leave the basket outside your invited guests' stalls in a place where horses can't reach.

WHOA:
Remember at any party, limit the amount of treats your horse eats.

Cock 'tail' & Potluck Buffet

Invite everyone to bring either a human or horse treat. Everyone can nibble buffet style. Remember manners—don't let your horse take over the entire table and gorge himself!

Kentucky Derby Party

Set up a TV in the barn and set up chairs for your guests. Serve mint julips to adults and green kool aid to kids. For horses, mix fove alfalfa cubes, one cup warm water, three tablespoons of corn oil, and a handful of sweet feed together in their feed buckets. Watch the Kentucky Derby with the horses. Observe any reactions from horses watching the races.

Claremont Stables, on 86th Street and Amsterdam Avenue in New York City, planned a retirement party for Legend. He retired to a farm in upstate New York. Boxes of tissues were provided! School horses are so deserving—anything you can do for them is always appreciated!
—Photos contributed by Claremont Stables of New York, NY.

Part of the your wedding party? Of course, Mariah is a bridesmaid!
—Photo contributed by Lisa Miller of Corrales, NM.

Encourage small informal gatherings—any time!
—Photo contributed by Terry Worthley of Monson, MA.

Super Suggestions:

❤ **Mix good deeds with good fun.** Plan a bran mash party at a local retired horse facility, such as Ryerss Farm for Aged Equines in Pennsylvania or another horse facility. Volunteer with friends to make and serve 20 - 30 bran mashes.

❤ **Say goodbye to good friends.** Plan a gathering, or even a roast, for a retiring school horse where everyone can tell stories about their memorable show or lesson experiences with the horse.

❤ **Introduce the newest star of the stable.** Plan a party where all your friends meet your new horse or foal.

❤ **Treat yourself and your horse to a true indulgence.** Plan a party where you hire an equine <u>and</u> human massage therapist. Why should the horses get all the pampering?

Games!

Pregnant Mare "Big or Bigger" Belly Game

Materials:
> White string
> Magic markers (a different color
> for each player)

Players first cut a piece of string long enough to fit clearly around the mare at her most pregnant spot, plus several extra feet (don't wrap it around the horse—just estimate). Let each player mark on the string how big they think the mare is at her most pregnant roundness. When each player has marked a spot, measure the mare with the string. Winner gets a free mucking from the losers! You can play this game every few weeks as the pregnant mare grows.

The New Horse (or Foal) Name Game

Materials:
> Thesaurus
> Paper
> Scissors
> Empty jar (or bowl)

Cut several sheets of paper into pieces about one inch by three inches. On each piece, have participants write a word or name that could be part of your new horse's name, and drop it into the jar.

When the jar is full, take turns pulling out two or three pieces at a time and combining those words in different ways to come up with names. After each round, return the pieces to the jar for the next player. Be sure to write down all the ideas that come up—by the time you're finished, there will be too many combinations to remember!

Game tip: Be sure to include the mare's name and nickname in the mix (if her name is more than one word, break it up on different pieces of paper). Also add the stallion's name. And include other fun things you like: animals, flowers, your name or other human names, action verbs, adjectives, adverbs, and whatever else inspires you (a thesaurus could be helpful). Feel free to add wacky and outrageous words to the jar, just for the fun of it.

Bobbing for Apples

Use a brand-new, clean muck bucket (a feed bucket is too small) filled to the brim with water. Drop in about 10 apples. Lead each horse to bucket and let them bob.

—*Contributed by June Laughlin of Bedford, VA. Humans can bob for apples too, if they don't mind the slobber the horses leave behind.*

Let your horse bob for sliced apples right in his own water bucket.

—*Contributed by Margaret Holzacker of East Hampton, NY. She lets her horse, Killarney County Kerry, bob for apples in the winter to encourage him to drink more water!*

Hide & Seek Treat Hunt

Cut up carrots into four-inch pieces and hide them deep inside a flake of hay. Your horse will have a terrific time grazing for them.

Or, hide carrots and about 4 - 5 hay cubes around his stall and paddock. It will keep him busy and he'll love the reward.

—Contributed by Sarah Battles of New City, NY.

Or, when hand grazing horses, hide carrots or alfalfa cubes in the grass. He can go in search of treats!

—Contributed by Dezi Kirsch of Frankfort, IL.

Mary Ellen's Corner
I hide Mary Ellen's treat in her window box (page 99) and sneak treats into a flake of hay! When hiding treats in your horse's stall or paddock, make sure the area is clean, and free of manure and dirt.

Hide 'em – Find 'em Easter Egg Hunt

Materials:
  Hard boiled eggs
  Easter egg coloring
  Paint brushes
  Egg cartons

The night before the egg hunt, throw an egg-coloring party for all the participants. Either soak the eggs in coloring or paint undiluted colors right onto them. When dry, pack the eggs back into the cartons and refrigerate.

The next morning, a designated Easter rabbit horse and rider hides the eggs in the fields and forest along the trail — on the ground, on tree limbs, in shallow streams, on rocks and boulders, even hanging from tree branches (using long strips of tape).

After the eggs are hidden, each rider takes along an empty egg carton to hold the eggs in a totebag or saddlebag. The rider returning after a prescribed amount of time with the most eggs wins.

—Contributed by Fay Seltzer of Happy Trails Western Wear & Horse Supplies, Leesport, PA. Fay leads the Reddale Valley Pony Club of Eastern Pennsylvania.

Designated egg-hider? —Photo contributed by Michelle Simpson of Claremore, OK.

Party Idea: Try decorating the eggs red and green for a Christmas Egg Trail Hunt or red, white and blue for a Fourth of July Hunt.

Add Points: For a more competitive egg hunt, mark the eggs 1, 2, or 3 depending on the difficulty of the hiding spot. The rider with the most points (not necessarily eggs) wins.

Helpful Hint:
Eggs hunts are fun even if it isn't Easter! They're safe if they are accidentally stepped on and it doesn't matter if a few of them are never found. The local raccoons and skunks won't mind!

141

Awaiting awards ceremony. —Photo contributed by Suzanne Drnec of Hobby Horse Clothing Company, Chino, CA. Photo by Stuart Veste.

Ultimate

GIFTS & PRIZES

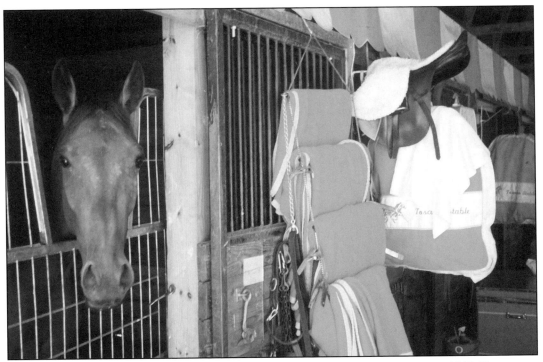

"Last Christmas, he got a travel toothbrush and toothpaste!" —Contributed by Catherine McHaffie of Springfield, MO. She hangs a Christmas stocking on her horse's stall on December 1st and every one in the barn gives him something. —Photo contributed by Jim Kersbergen of Hoboken, NJ. An eager Standardbred awaits his treat at Showplace Farms in Freehold, NJ.

Party Gifts & Game Prizes

Some ideas for party gifts and prizes—

1) A gift certificate to a local tack or feedstore.

2) New feed or water buckets.

3) Bucket of apples tied with a pretty bow!

4) 50 pounds of carrots delivered to the barn.

5) A new feed bucket stuffed full of store bought and homemade treats.

6) A decorative basket of horse cookies.

7) A snack bag that attaches to the saddle or breast collar, stuffed with treats.

8) A timothy and alfalfa hay bouquet. (Pick through several bales of hay and bunch together the prettiest and choicest pieces. Tie together with a piece of long, thin licorice.)

9) Disposable cameras so everyone has a chance to take party pictures.

Is it something for us? —Photo contributed by Debbie McLeod of The Book Tree, Lenexa, KS.

10) Picture frames (for favorite party pictures).

11) All new brushes!

12) A water bucket stuffed full of bathing supplies.

13) Towels ranging in size from wash cloth to bath-size. Chamois cloths, too.

14) A leather halter and leadline with brass shank.

15) Personalized nameplates for everything, from stall doors and halters to tack trunks and feed buckets.

16) Small bucket stuffed full of leather cleaning supplies.

Super Suggestion:

Don't forget "Just because" gifts for:

- Deserving grooms
- Moms or friends who help at horse shows
- Friends who muck while you are away
- School horses who are very deserving
- Fathers who listen and listen, over and over again, to everything the horse has done
- Brothers who have to fix stall doors and broken pipes!
- To families who have helped you shovel in load after load of sawdust, or stack bales of hay
- The veterinarian who comes immediately for every bump and scrape
- The feed and hay man who drops everything to deliver your feed
- The farrier who patiently trims and shoes inpatient horses
- Parents who have to jump up from breakfast to chase loose horses
- Boyfriends and husbands who now know they are relegated to second and possibly even third.

145

Gifts & Prizes

17) Homemade tack box cedar sachets. (Buy a pair of children's pink socks with lace at the top. Fill with cedar and tie shut with a satin ribbon.)

18) A certificate that entitles the bearer to a free stall mucking, tack cleaning, or horse laundry washing.

19) A donation to a local horse rescue operation in the name of the honored guest.

20) Sponsorship of a horse at a retired facility or horse rescue in name of the honoree!

21) T-shirts made up for everyone marking the party occasion.

22) Horse books or a subscription to any horse magazine.

23) Hire a professional equine photographer to take portraits.

24) *The Ultimate Guide to Pampering Your Horse* or *The Original Book of Horse Treats*, of course!

—Compiled with help from Darlene Williams of Green Valley Tack, Pine Island, NY.

Certificate of Mucking

This certificate entitles the bearer

_____

(said owner of dirty stall)

to a free Major Mucking by me

_____

(said mucker)

on any day that they choose! I will fulfill my part of the deal by completely picking out every last poop and piling the stall high with fresh bedding!

Signed

_____

(said mucker)

Certificates make a great gift. They're inexpensive and can mean a lot to the recipient! Photocopy this certificate or create your own for other tasks such as grooming, feeding, waiting for the vet or blacksmith, sweeping cobwebs, or tack cleaning.

Pregnant Mare Watch Certificate

I, _____ (said mare watcher)

do hereby give one full night or whatever time is needed

that is equal to one full night to oversee, _____ , (said mare).

I will prepare my own coffee and relieve, _____ , (said mare owner).

Just call me, anytime—day or even night.

Signed _____

(said mare watcher)

Howdy, the seahorse, bedecked in a shell encrusted bridle accented with green and purple ribbons. The mermaid wears a gold bathing suit adorned with sea shells covered by a gold lame cape with ribbons and gold tassels. —Photo contributed by Shirley Gough of Versailles, KY. Being an experienced side saddle rider is the only way Shirley can ride in this costume. Shirley is a costumer designer and creator for the Kentucky Horse Park's Parade of Champions.

Ultimate
COSTUMES

*Bring on the clowns. —Photos contributed by Eloise King-Pinkel
of Rancho Santa Fe, CA. This is about the best clown costume I have seen!
Above left and above: Gindari, a 23-year-old Arabian, is a Grand Prix level
Dressage horse. Whether you are a 4-H'er, Grand Prix level Dressage, or
Reining champion, anyone can have fun and dress up!*

Costumes

Dressing up your horse is truly a do-it-yourself exercise in creativity, limited in scope only by your horse's level of patience (or lack thereof). If you're blessed with a horse who will gladly tolerate any indignity your fertile mind can dream up, then costuming possibilities are endless. With a more sensitive horse, however, be sure to exercise your good judgment and slowly accustom him to the costume before you expect him to dress up and party!

Delta as a unicorn. You might consider stapling a third piece of ribbon to the bottom of the unicorn so it can tie to the crown piece of the halter for more stability.

Unicorn

Materials:

> Poster board
> Scotch tape
> Pink tempera paint
> Paint brushes
> Glitter
> Elmer's glue
> Pink satin ribbon
> Cardboard

Roll poster board into a tight cone about 8 inches long and tape the seam closed. Decorate with paint and glue on glitter and let dry. Then staple a piece of satin ribbon to each side of the cone long enough to tie around horse's head. Cover the staples with tape.

Then cut a circle out of cardboard about 2 - 3 inches in diameter and tape it flat to the bottom of the cone. This helps the unicorn to stay upright when it is tied to the horse's head.

For Frilly Extras: Braid satin ribbon into the mane and tail. Sprinkle glitter into his coat over his hindquarters.

Add Wings: Make wings from cardboard painted white to turn your horse into Pegasus.

Super Suggestions:

- ❤ **Check in with the pros.** Fabric and craft stores will have supplies and perhaps horse costume ideas, as well, if you don't mind getting funny looks for asking. Your tack store might have information about about costume classes, and could also be a goldmine for ideas.

- ❤ **Costume on the cheap.** Shop garage sales and thrift stores for old dresses, bonnets, and men's pants in size XXXL (get ready for sympathetic looks if you buy a pair of these).

- ❤ **Use washable paint.** Only use water-based, non-toxic paint on horses. It's easiest to wash off! Try tempera paint, a safe children's paint.

- ❤ **Twist 'em up.** Use sandwich bags twist-ties to tie costumes to your horse's mane, tail or bridle. Available in boxes of sandwich bags or garbage bags.

- ❤ **Incorporate hard hats in all costumes.** If you are riding, make sure you include a hard hat for safety! (Horses may be a bit nervous of the costumes.)

Arabian costume.
—Photo contributed by Mary Jane Ciraco of
Morning Mist Farm, Deland, FL.

Arabian costume. —Photo contributed by Jam Tepoel of Tazewell, VA.

Baghdad Genie Princess. —Photo contributed by Janice Elsishans
of Oak Ridge, NJ. Her especially calm Arabian will allow her to carry
an umbrella for a truly royal effect!

Costumes

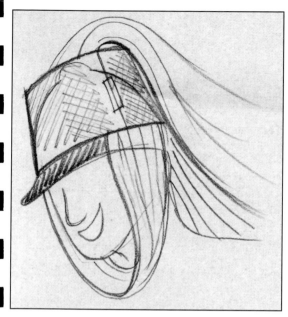

Make a Genie hat.
Simply loop the fabric through the hat
and slip it onto your head over the hard hat.

WHOA:
Whenever riding, always wear a hard hat. Although many of the pictures in this section show people without one, <u>always</u> adjust your costume accordingly to include one—no matter what.

Before hopping on your horse with your newly made costume, let him see it first and get used to the swirling fabric. Same goes for his costume, too!

And remember to make sure all loose pieces are tied securely and won't come loose to frighten your horse!

Baghdad Genie Princess

Materials:

> Brightly colored sheer fabric
> Matching heavier weight fabric
> Black velvet
> Large fancy gold tassels
> Fancy fringe
> Black poster board
> Gold magic marker or paint
> Gold glitter and beads
> Shoe laces (try to find a pair of flashy gold-speck laces)

Make a Breast Plate Necklace: Cut about 1 - 2 yards of black velvet and roll it together with the same amount of sheer fabric. Cut a hole in each end and string shoe laces through. Tie it together and then lace the "necklace" to the dee rings on an English saddle or to the horn of a western. Tie tassels to the front and sides. This breast plate is for adornment only and it should fit loosely.

Quarter Sheet: Cut enough of the heavier fabric so that it will hang over your saddle and horse's rump. Sew fringe on three sides and decorate with gold paint and beads. Drape it over the saddle and your horse's rump, and simply sit on it to hold it in place.

Bridle Decoration: Hang tassles on each side of your bridle. Stretch one yard of sheer fabric along the reins and tie it to the reins with tassels.

Your Costume: Simply wrap several yards of the sheer fabric around your waist and fasten it with safety pins. Decorate a black turtle neck, which you will tuck into the skirt, with shiny beads and dots of gold magic marker, paint, or even glue on gold glitter. Or look for a long, flowing dress at garage sales or thrift shops. If you find one, match all the fabric to this dress color.

To Make Your Hat: Cut a piece of poster board in a rectangle wide enough to go around your head and hard hat, and about six inches high. Tape it together to make a cylinder that will fit around your head, and trim away any excess. Decorate with a gold marker, and glue on glitter and beads. Cut about 2 - 3 yards of sheer fabric and loop it through the hat. (See diagram.) The loop goes under your chin with the fabric spilling out of the posterboard cap and cascading down your back. Staple it to the hat to keep it in place.

—Based on a picture (see page 152) contributed by Janice Elsishans of Oak Ridge, NJ.

153

Grim Reaper with skeleton. Ed, an American Saddlebred, was painted with water-based paint directly on to his coat. —Contributed by Shirley Gough of Versailles, KY. —Photo contributed by Mary Sauer.

Punkin's award-winning skeleton costume.
—Contributed by Resa Webber of Oakfield Farm, Center Point, TX.
—Photo contributed by DALCO.

Costumes

Skeleton

Materials:

- Sleazy Sleepwear Sheet
- Sleazy Hood
- Grease pencil
- Paint
- Paint brushes—several sizes
- Two pairs of sweat pants
- Sweat shirt
- Safety pins

Preparation: First, dress your horse in the Sleazy, using a hood and body sheet to cover the horse as completely as possibly. (The Sleazy Sleepwear is available in assorted colors. Try to match your horse to their color or dye a silver Sleazy to get the exact color you want.)

Cut the sweat pants in half, straight up through the crotch. (They should match the color of the Sleazy. Dye white ones to match.) Pull each one onto your horse's leg so that the elastic ankle part is around the pastern just under the ankle. Pull them up and safety pin them to the Sleazy sheet. (For safety, pin them so the point of the pin opens outward!)

For the tail, cut an arm out of a matching sweat shirt and sew one end shut. Slip the tail into the sleeve and pin it to the Sleazy sheet.

Initial Sketch: Using the grease pencil, sketch an outline of the bones directly onto the fabric while the horse is still wearing the costume. Refer to an anatomy book if necessary to reproduce the proper bone structure.

Then, remove the costume carefully (so as not to smudge the outline). Don't forget to unpin the sweat pants before removing the Sleazy. Lay everything flat and paint in the skeleton outline, using an opaque paint. (Use white non-toxic paint for dark colored Sleazies or black non-toxic paint for light colored costumes. Or try flourescent paint for glow-in-the-dark fun!)

Costume tip: When placing the costume on your horse's head, put the bridle on first. Use only the crown piece (or head stall) and bit (no nose or brow band). If your horse will stand it, use the crown piece to hold his ears down. Then, slip the Sleazy over. This will give the illusion of no ears, like a real skeleton.

Your Costume: Make a sweat suit outfit for yourself complete with painted ribs and bones like your horse. Purchase a plastic skull face mask to finish the picture.

—*Contributed by Resa Webber of Oakfield Farm, Center Point, TX. Her horse, Punkin, has won costume classes two years in a row.*

Costume tip: It's best to ride this costume bareback. If you are unsure of your seat, however, sneak a saddle under the Sleazy.

Costume tip: You can always create this costume by painting directly onto your horse—but remember to use only water-based, non-toxic tempera paint. (I had a friend who didn't use water-based paint. She was washing her horse for weeks and finally had to wait until the paint wore off!)

WHOA:
Remember, costumes should only be put on patient horses. Never force a horse into wearing something he doesn't want. Try the costume on a school horse who would probably love the attention!

Remember to be careful if you place the bridle over their ears. Some horses will not like this. If yours doesn't, just leave his ears out.

Also, again, use water-based, non-toxic paint only. I like the Sleazy part of this costume because it may be too cold to bathe a horse after a Halloween costume class or party in late October.

Costumes

Zebra & Jungle Woman (or Man)

Materials:

- Tempera or water-based paint
- Paint brushes—several sizes
- Chalk
- Fake vines from a craft store

Preparation: Purchase black water-based paint and chalk for white or grey horses, or white water-based paint and chalk for dark colored horses.

Using a photo of a zebra as a reference, draw an outline of the stripes onto your horse with chalk first. Then, fill the outlines in with paint. Bring along extra carrots to mollify a ticklish horse.

Costume tips: Instead of painting directly on your horse, follow the Skeleton costume directions and paint a Sleazy sheet and hood instead. This is a good idea if the weather is too cool for bathing.

Costume tips: Or leave your horse unpainted. Just adorn a saddlepad with leaves and vines for a jungle-like appearance.

Make Your Own Jungle Costume: For real authenticity, purchase leather-like material or fake suede and fashion a loin cloth dress. (See diagram at right). Measure yourself from the top of your shoulder to your knee. Multiply that length by two. This gives you the amount of the fabric you will need.

Lay the material out flat and at the very center, cut a hole large enough for your head to poke through. Then, just to the right and left of the hole gather the fabric and tie it with baling twine. These are your shoulders. Then, fold the dress in half, slip it over your head. Your arms slip through the openings at the sides under the baling twine ties. Tie it closed at the waist with more baling twine and twist in the vines as an added touch.

Or Simply Wear a Bathing Suit: Tie the plastic vine around your waist as a belt! Or use real vines from around your barn (make sure they are not poison ivy).

WHOA:
This costume requires you to paint directly on the horse. Make sure you buy non-toxic, water-based paint such as tempera paint. Also, test it first to make sure it will wash out after it has been dried on for several hours.

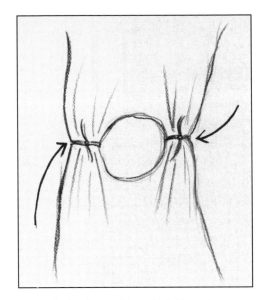

Gather the shoulders with baling twine.

Prepared jungle costume. It is rather becoming!

Santa Claus and reindeer. —Photo contributed by
Tiffany Magnett of Lexington, KY.

Wicked witches. —Photo contributed by
Eloise King-Pinkel of Rancho Santa Fe, CA.

The Burger King. —Photo contributed by
Marcy Gamester of Westford, MA.

Santa and Mrs. Claus. —Photo contributed by
Adele Bailey of Fox Cry Farm, Conowingo, MD.

Super Suggestions:

♥ **Put their best feet forward.** For fabulous looking hooves, paint with hoof dressing or acrylic hoof polish and sprinkle on glitter. Try glow-in-the-dark glitter for an eerie effect! —*Contributed by Shirley Gough of Versailles, KY.*

♥ **Stencil on glitter designs.** For something different, use a stencil to apply glitter hip checkers, quarter marks, and even hearts, stars and moons! —*Contributed by Shirley Gough of Versailles, KY. There is a very washable children's paste (Elmer's Sno-Drift Paste) that you can paint right on the horse through a stencil. I tested it on Mary Ellen and it washed right off even though it had been on for hours.*

♥ **Sprinkle on the gold dust.** Sprinkle glitter in his coat and costume for a shimmering effect. Keep it away from his face and eyes.

♥ **Mask that marvel.** For a quick masked avenger look, try an old race horse hood! —*Contributed by J. Burns of Hoboken, NJ.*

*Above left and above: Two generations of bathing beauties.
Note the flippers tied to only the most patient horse's legs!
—Photos contributed by Linda Abrams of Milner, GA.*

*The Horse Motivator. Note the fishing pole which has a carrot dangling in front of the horse—
the motivator! Bring along extra carrots to reward the horse outfitted like this.*

Costumes

Rabbit & Carrot

Materials:

> White terry cloth fabric
> Pink fabric
> Pink tempera paint
> Pillow stuffing
> Pipe cleaners
> Straw hat (optional)
> Orange sweat suit
>   (shirt and pants)
> Brown magic marker
> Plastic green plant
> Old hard hat with a plug at top
> Duct tape

To Make a Rabbit Out of Your Horse: Cut out large rabbit ears from the terry cloth material and sew them together. Stitch pink fabric to the front to resemble ear openings. Sew the ears right to the bridle. These are floppy ears that will hang down.

Once the bridle is on the horse, twist pipe cleaners to the nose band for rabbit whiskers. Paint a pink triangle in between for a rabbit nose. As a finishing touch,

Silly rabbit! Treats are for horses.
(Mary Ellen <u>does</u> look like a rabbit.)

ball up pillow stuffing and attach it to your horse's tail with twist ties. Option: add a straw hat to his head, cutting holes for his ears.

Your Costume: Draw brown magic marker stripes horizontally across the entire orange sweat suit to resemble carrot lines. Remove the plug at the top of an old hard hat. Press the plastic plant into the hole and secure it on the inside with

Delta as a rabbit. Try a craft store for premade rabbit ears—they may actually be cheaper. —Photo contributed by Judy Decker of Johnson, NY.

duct tape. Make a cushion out of padding and duct tape between the person's head and the plastic plant for comfort.

—Contributed by Kristy Bruns of Prairie Song Designs, Valley Center, KS.

Costume Tip: To make the ears stand upright, sew a wire frame into the rabbit ears. Bend a flexible, but strong wire into the ear shape you wish. Cut the fabric into that shape, allowing a little extra at the edges. Sew the wire and fabric together by folding the fabric edge over the wire. Leave a little extra wire peeking out at the bottom to wrap around a bridle or halter.

159

Costume Ideas:

- ❤ Secretariat and jockey
- ❤ Christmas elf
- ❤ Romeo and Juliet
- ❤ Witches, warlocks and magicians
- ❤ Santa Claus and Rudolph
- ❤ Blues Brothers
- ❤ Princess and serf
- ❤ Stegosaurus
- ❤ Hobo and police man
- ❤ John Wayne
- ❤ Trigger and Roy Rogers
- ❤ Lone Ranger & Tonto
- ❤ Nurse and hospital victim. —*Contributed by Karen Ufret of Port Jervis, NY.*
- ❤ Black Beauty
- ❤ Large baby in big diapers
- ❤ Calamity Jane and Buffalo Bill
- ❤ Sheriff Wyatt Earp and The Clanton gang

Costumes

Lady Godiva

Following in the tradition of Lady Godiva's famous ride, wear only a tan colored body suit and an extra long wig. Of course, include shoes with heels and a hard hat!

Farmer & Accompanying Haystack

Dress your horse in an old horse sheet and sew pieces of hay all over it to resemble a haystack. You, the farmer, wear overalls with patches at the knees and a straw hat.

—*Contributed by Ashley Hammond of Ontario, Canada.*

The Frito Bandito. —Photo contributed by Linda Abrams of Milner, GA.

Farmer & Hay Bale

Buy extra, extra large overalls. Cut the seat and back out so they will fit onto your horse's chest and front legs. Sew on additional straps to make them stay on. Add a straw hat for the horse's head with holes cut for his ears. Your horse—the farmer.

Find a sturdy cardboard box. Cut two holes on each side of a box for your arms to poke through and one for your head at the top. Glue hay to all sides and for authenticity, attach some baling twine. Either lead your horse or ride in the saddle. You—the hay bale!

The Masked Avenger. —Photo contributed by Udell and Lynn Ingles of Sorento, Il.

Navaho Pony

Materials:

> Red and yellow tempera paint
> Baling twine
> Indian blanket
> Feathers - colored or natural

Paint red and yellow Indian war paint directly onto your horse and drape an Indian blanket over his back (or cover the saddle). Fashion a bridle out of baling twine to look like an old Indian bridle, and attach baling twine reins to a nose loop. Use sandwich bag twist ties to attach feathers to the mane, tail and bridle. (see photo at right.)

—Contributed by Rosemary Speakes of West Milton, OH.

Sooner in an Indian Pony outfit.—Photo contributed by Rosemary Speake of West Milton, OH.

Zorro. —Photo contributed by Michelle Simpson of Claremore, OK.

Ride 'em cowboy! —Photo contributed by Udell and Lynn Ingles of Sorento, Il.

Ghost. —Photo contributed by Michelle Simpson of Claremore, OK. Note: the horse in the background, upper left. With his back turned, he seems not to notice a ghost in the paddock!

Many horses will understandably balk at something this silly. Delta, however, takes everything in stride.

161

Make a knight costume with aluminum foil and a fly mask.—Photo contributed by Mary Ann O'Keefe of Whip N Spur Catalog & Tack Shop, Tampa, FL.

From the Parade of Champions at the Kentucky Horse Park comes the Medieval Knight and his horse. —Contributed by Shirley Gough of Versailles, KY. —Photo contributed by Debby Prewitt. We recommend visiting the beautiful Kentucky Horse Park, located in the heart of Kentucky horse country just north of Lexington.

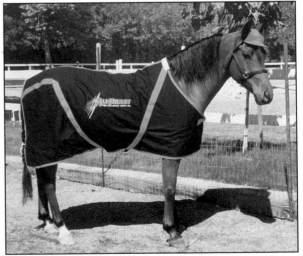

If not dressed up in costume, at least dress up to promote your business. Chadwick promotes the family's electric supply company.—Photo contributed by Jackie Hahn-Winans of Northridge, CA.

Costumes

Rolling the dice. —Photo contributed by Linda Abrams of Milner, GA.

Movie star or beach bunny? —Photo contributed by Sandy Larkin of Webster, NY.

A dainty Ballerina. —Photo contributed by Linda Abrams of Milner, GA. A little heart has been trimmed into hair on pony's rump.

Aladdin and his lamp.—Photo contributed by Elizabeth Sutton of Charlottesville, VA.

Author's note:
I would love to see pictures of your horse all dressed up in the costumes you make! Perhaps we can use them in upcoming books and newsletters. Send any photos to: June Evers, Box 456, Goshen, NY 10924.

Costume Ideas:

❤ Plow horse and farmer

❤ Cow and milker with stool

❤ Make a bay horse a pinto with water base paint

❤ If you dare, make a grey horse— hot pink. **Remember:** Use only non-toxic water-based colorings that easily rinse out! Test them first to make sure.

❤ Bride and groom

❤ Flower power hippie horse, with tie-dyed accessories

❤ Wall Street stock broker, complete with pinstriped suit

❤ Carousel horse

❤ Headless horseman. —*Contributed by Resa Webber of Oakfield Farm, Center Point, TX.*

❤ A rodeo clown with bull complete with horns and mooing voice box. —*Contributed by Shirley Gough of Versailles, KY.*

❤ Robin Hood and Maid Marion

❤ Little Red Riding Hood and wolf

❤ Napoleon

Layla and Vigil Mite. —Photo contributed by Susanna Brandon, editor and publisher of The Stable Companion, Indianapolis, IN.

Showing in style: Ashley, Amy and Cinnabuns. —Contributed by Kathy Cline of West Palm Beach, FL. —Photo contributed by O'Neill.

Just plan a play day for goofing off! —Contributed by Moira Harris, editor of Horse Illustrated, Mission Viejo, CA. —Photo contributed by Kendra Bond of Buzzards Bay, MA.

Norwegian Fjord, Kaiser, and Jenny Robinson at the Carriage Classic (passenger Jill Ryder). —Photo contributed by Ronni Robinson of Pony Tracks Gallery, Olivos, CA.

This schedule features a full day of activities. Mix, match and add ideas of your own to make your pampering day special. Be sure to keep to his regular feed schedule!

Schedule

8:00 **Breakfast:** Top off his normal breakfast with a special Alfalfa Bloom Salad (page 75).

9:00 **Turnout:** Generously apply Apple Cider Bug-Be-Gone (see page 119). Attach a fringed fly bonnet to your horse's leather halter for extra protection.

9:15 **Housekeeping:** Deep clean his stall and set up as an Imperial Deluxe Suite. He deserves it! (Page 101.)

10:45 **Morning treat:** Surprise him in the field with a delectable treat served on a silver platter. Try the Bundled Carrot Twigs on page 70.

11:15 **Hoof pampering:** Clean and check each foot extra carefully. Then smear on (if you dare) the All-Natural Bacon Grease treatment. (Page 39.)

12:00 **Lunch or treat:** Mix his lunch with warm water or, if he doesn't normally get lunch, serve Glazed Hay Knots from page 73.

12:30 **Facial:** Start with a brushing session to work out the dirt, and include a facial massage to help relax your horse. Then finish up with a Warm Winter Facial (or a cool one in summer). See pages 22 and 23.

1:30 **Body massage:** Treat him to a full massage (page 114). Pay additional attention to the muscles of back and hindquarters (page 19).

2:30 **Grooming:** Pay particular attention to any itchy spots that need tending. Thoroughly brush his mane and tail. Try the End of Tail Scrubby (page 28). And don't forget the satisfaction check on page 113.

"I try to make Sundays special for Heemer and myself. I plan the day with things he enjoys and I am happier for the time I've spent with him!" —Contributed by Lynda Hamilton of Santa Rosa, CA.

Miss Merry Legs. —Photo contributed by Kara Donovan of Chester, NJ.

Super Suggestions:

- **Stock up on the necessities of life.** The day before your pampering day, visit your local tack store and replenish all supplies you'll need, and purchase any new brush, toy, or treats that you would like to try.

- **Keep mealtimes regular.** Special days are always fun, but remember to stick to your horse's regular feed schedule.

- **Don't forget the others.** Set aside Saturday to groom the entire herd of turned out horses who don't normally get daily attention.
  —*Contributed by Eileen Mestas of Rancho de Caballos, Boone, CO.*

*Even I should get some pampering!
—Photo contributed by Meredith Woundy-Williams of Lexington Horse & Country, Lexington, VA. Queensburro the donkey was adopted by Meredith from the U.S. Bureau of Land Management.*

166

Schedule

2:45 Riding session

3:45 Cooling out: Take your time and walk him for a long time, letting him graze on tender tidbits outside his paddock.

4:30 Bathing session: The Sudsy 6-Step Bathing Beauty Basics, of course. (If it's warm enough.) Then apply a misting of fly spray.

5:00 Party: Throw an Instant Aisle Party right in the barn (see Super Suggestion on page 131). Just serve a small amount of treats so it won't spoil his dinner.

6:00 Dinner: At the party or in his stall, prepare a Sweet & Soupy Bran Mash (page 59) with a sliced carrot. (Or serve his regular feed.)

8:00 Evening check: Just refresh his water and do a Quickie Fluff & Muck in his stall (page 104) before he goes to bed.

9:00 *Tuck in and say goodnight . . .*

Cooling out at the choicest grass. —Photo contributed by Kim Cassidy of Middletown, NJ.

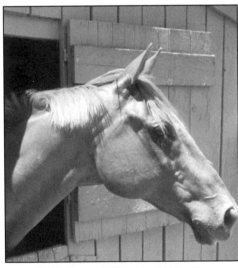

The last haying at 9:00 PM is their "cookies and milk" before bedtime. —Contributed by Donna Tredway of New Smyrna, FL. —Photo contributed by Bonnie Scribner of Mineral, VA.

...with a Hug and a Kiss on the Nose!

Ladybug. —Photo contributed by Shannon Lubben of Gilman, IL.

A Quarter Horse named Desire.—Photo contributed by Rosemary Speakes of Blue Haven Farm, West Milton, OH.

Mary Ellen and me. —Photo contributed by Judy Decker of Johnson, NY.

—Photo contributed by The American Morgan Horse Association of Shelburne, VT.

—Photo contributed by Suzanne Drnec of Hobby Horse Clothing Company, Chino, CA.

Write Us!

Be included in our other books:
Do you have any recipes, grooming tips or handy hints, home remedies, costumes, unique trick you've taught your horse, or just comments you'd like to share? Drop us a note, we might use it in an upcoming book!

Send along funny pictures of your horse
that we can use in upcoming books and newsletters.

Want to drop a note to the author?
Send it to June V. Evers at the address below.

Look for other Horse Hollow Press books
at your local tack store: *The Original Book of Horse Treats* (a cookbook of horse treats), *The Incredible Little Book of 10,001 Names for Horses* (a listing of literally thousands of names) and our newest book: *Horse Lover's Birthday Book* (a book of days to remember as well as a guide to gifts for horses and humans you can make yourself).

Write for our free catalog of products
and books for horse lovers.

Visit our website: www.horsehollowpress.com

HORSE HOLLOW PRESS, Inc.
P.O. Box 456, Goshen, NY 10924-0456
www.horsehollowpress.com
e-mail: info@horsehollowpress.com

To order more copies, photocopy this page and mail to the address below. Or, visit your favorite tack & feed store!

Yes! I want to order more books. Please send me:

QTY:

_____ *The Original Book of Horse Treats.* Hardcover wire-o-binding. $19.95
Cookbook of horse treats.

_____ *The Ultimate Guide to Pampering Your Horse.* Hardcover wire-o-binding. $24.95
Hundreds of pampering tips and handy hints to please your horse.

_____ *The Incredible Little Book of 10,001 Names for Horses.* Paperback. $8.95
Literally thousands of names for horses and ponies.

_____ *Horse Lover's Birthday Book.* Paperback. $4.95
A book of days to remember as well as a guide to gifts for horses and humans you can make yourself.

I have included $4.95 for shipping & packing. Pay only one price for shipping, no additional needed for more books ordered. (If you are ordering only the *Horse Lover's Birthday Book*, only include .75 cents shipping. It is a lightweight book.)

TOTAL ENCLOSED: $_____ (Check, money order, or credit cards accepted. NY residents, please add sales tax.)

OR CALL TOLL-FREE: 1-800-4-1-HORSE to order!

Mary Ellen Says: *Tell your friends about this book! Stop by your local tack store to buy more copies or order from us!*

Name: _____

Address: _____

City/State/Zip:_____

Phone:_____

Visa/MC/AMEX: _____ Exp. Date:_____

Signature: _____